THE DIMENSIONS
OF COMPARATIVE
LIBRARIANSHIP

THE DIMENSIONS
OF COMPARATIVE
LIBRARIANSHIP

J. Periam Danton

American Library Association
Chicago 1973

Z
665
.D23

Library of Congress Cataloging in Publication Data

Danton, J   Periam, 1908–
  The dimensions of comparative librarianship.

  Bibliography: p.
  1. Comparative librarianship.   I. Title.
Z665.D23   020   73-7935
ISBN 0-8389-0154-9

                      Printed in the United States of America

To my doctoral students,
especially the members of
"Comparative Librarianship,"
whose often troublesome questions
provided some of the challenge
for undertaking this study.

Contents

Preface

Since 1961 I have had responsibility for a doctoral seminar in "Comparative Librarianship" at the School of Librarianship of the University of California, Berkeley. My reading and other preparations for the seminar, the discussions that have taken place and questions that have been raised at its many meetings, and my reflections on the state of the art, particularly when contrasted with other disciplines, have led to an increasingly strong conviction that comparative study in librarianship is sadly deficient in a number of major respects.

This essay attempts to describe and demonstrate the deficiencies, suggest the reasons for them, and propose amelioration; the avenues of inquiry are the fundamental elements of the area as noted in the Table of Contents.

Briefly summarized, it is the contention of this study—its hypotheses—that most of the literature described as "comparative librarianship" is thin, largely narrative and descriptive, and often neither comparative nor in conformity with even minimal standards of scholarly investigation; that among the reasons for this is the lack of (1) a precise, generally agreed upon terminology, (2) commonly accepted criteria for the evaluation of published studies, and (3) any considerable number of qualified investigators. A possible cause of this last is the fact that no library education program anywhere has developed comparative studies as a major teaching and research field. It is further contended that the scope of the area has not been delineated, and that a consistent and defensible methodology has been lacking. A very large proportion of what has been produced, even when not purely narrative and descriptive, has been innocent of explicitly stated hypotheses, clearly defined concepts and variables, recognition of stated and unstated assumptions, and announcement of the minimum standards of proof acceptable as validation of the hypotheses.

Much of this, perhaps all of it, is scarcely to be wondered at. Comparative studies in other fields and, indeed, the fields themselves in their beginnings, faced uncertainty and confusion concerning concepts, terminology, scope, goals and purposes, and methodology. This was true of anthropology, business administration, economics, education, political science, psychology, and sociology. So far as comparative work is concerned, it is to a certain extent still true of some of them. It would be extraordinary if our infant, comparative librarianship, were an exception.

The data to test my hypotheses are not equally abundant, precise, and clear-cut. I have collected such data as are available—in some cases a sampling—but recognize that what I have been able to accomplish does not unarguably test all of the hypotheses. I believe, however, that sufficient data are presented to provide presumptive evidence in support of all of them.

Throughout much of the work, I have relied heavily upon the experience and findings of other disciplines, particularly in the social sciences, and most especially in education, for data to support the hypotheses. I have done so simply because, at many points, no other kinds of evidence are available. The reliance upon education is heaviest for two reasons: first, because this discipline, as discussed in chapter 1, is most nearly akin to librarianship; and second, because comparativists in education have in recent years wrestled with precisely the same problems and questions that are the concern of this study. For example, my manuscript notes tell me that I provisionally decided upon the title, *The Dimensions of Comparative Librarianship*, in the spring of 1971. It was not until a year later that I came upon the article by Reginald Edwards, "The Dimensions of Comparison, and of Comparative Education" (*Comparative Education Review* 14:239–54 [Oct. 1970]).

In chapter 2, "The Dimensions of Terminology, Definition, and Scope," and in chapter 3, "The Dimensions of Purpose and Value," I have quoted very extensively, and far more so than was my inclination to do, from librarians who have written on these two topics. I have done so, however, not in an attempt to "appeal to authority"; on the contrary, I have found myself in disagreement with most of what has been written, believing it to be misleading, contradictory, unclear, incomplete, or downright false. My purpose in offering the reader this extensive documentation has been to persuade him that I have made an exhaustive canvass of our literature on the two topics and, by displaying that literature *in extenso*, to enable him to judge for himself the validity of my criticism and my generally different views.

The reader who is already acquainted with the development of comparative studies in other major fields, and is aware of the significant contributions which such studies have made (as well as of the lack of a corresponding development and contribution in librarianship), may wish to skip the introductory chapter, which is simply a brief summary of these two points.

Similarly, the reader familiar with the nature, importance, and values of scientific method, particularly as applied to the social sciences, is likely to find little that is new or of interest to him in chapter 5, "The Dimension of Methodology."

International cooperation and activity have been cardinal facts of life, particularly since the end of the Second World War, and bid fair to continue on a rising curve. The meaningful organization of libraries in the developing countries, and the intellectual progress of librarianship in the developed countries as well, are dependent to a large measure upon better understanding, particularly of understanding why things are as they are. Comparative librarianship provides a major avenue for bringing about such understanding.

It is my hope that this essay may serve as a beginning contribution toward the recognition of comparative librarianship as an important area for our attention and toward the founding of that area as a field of serious inquiry. I say "beginning" because, as I believe the data presented hereafter abundantly demonstrate, we are only now arriving at the outer threshold both of a recognition of the field and of serious work in it. Consequently, I confidently anticipate that others will take up, develop, and improve upon this effort as the result of our future experience. I am convinced that a major development in the field is necessary, and will become increasingly so, first as the historical separation between peoples further disappears and yields place to greater cooperative effort in all spheres of activity, including librarianship and, second, as our profession increasingly demands solid knowledge about its work.

I am greatly in debt to the following institutions and individuals:

The University of California, Berkeley, for a sabbatical leave which enabled me to spend an uninterrupted academic year on the project;

My colleagues at the School of Librarianship, University of California, whose work was certainly not lessened by my absence;

The John Simon Guggenheim Memorial Foundation for a generous award, 1971–72;

The chief administrative officers—deans, directors, heads, chairmen—of library schools, departments, chairs, institutes, and other library education agencies in many countries, who provided me with invaluable information and documentation, opportunities to talk to teaching colleagues, and, in numerous cases, warm hospitality;

Dr. Rudolph Fiedler, General-Director, Austrian National Library, and his colleagues, particularly Hofrat Dr. Franz Steininger, Chief of the Printed Book Collection, for study space in the library, the privilege of unusually generous access, and a co-operation which can fairly be described as unlimited in meeting my needs;

Mrs. Hermine Zahel of the Library's Interlibrary Loan Division, who served me most ably throughout the year as bibliographer and research assistant;

Miss Renate Barousch, Academic Translator (akad. Übersetzerin), my equally assiduous and helpful secretary;

Mrs. Susan Holmes Cavaliere, Mrs. Jean Helen Lyon, Miss Edith Ingrid Radkey, and Miss Annamarie Welteke, at various times students and research assistants in the School of Librarianship, University of California who, over the past few years, were enormously helpful to me in bibliographical compilation and analysis, and other kinds of reference work;

The very large number of writers on comparative studies, from several fields, especially education, law, linguistics, politics, religion, and sociology, who have stimulated my thinking, provided me with "leads," and helped to form my ideas; except in the introductory chapter, which summarizes well-known and readily verifiable fact, I have tried faithfully to record my indebtedness of this kind through the footnote references; and,

Finally, to that small group of thoughtful and questioning persons, to whom I have been happy to dedicate these pages.

I feel compelled to add a concluding note. Everyone who attempts to work in some depth in the field of comparative studies in general, and undertakes to review what has been written, must be filled with a kind of despair at the vastness of the literature available to him. It seems very doubtful to me that anyone could claim to "know" all of the comparative literature in any one of the major fields mentioned above, let alone that literature in all of them.[1] I have read, with varying degrees of thoroughness, about five hundred works; there are certainly five thousand or more which I have not read. Among these there are surely many important publications which I might have reviewed. To the authors of these—and to the reader—I express my regret.

Vienna, June, 1972

In the interest of historical accuracy I leave the foregoing as it was when I wrote it. I must now, however, additionally express my indebtedness to:

The Committee on Research of Berkeley's Academic Senate, for a grant to cover preparation and typing of the final manuscript;

My Berkeley colleagues, Professors Madison S. Beeler, Albert A. Ehrenzweig and Thomas W. Livingston, of the linguistics, law, and education faculties, respectively, for suggestions on the sections about comparative studies in those fields in chapter 1;

Professors Lester Asheim, Chicago, and Raynard C. Swank, Berkeley, and my wife whose critical reading of the entire manuscript provided me with many valuable suggestions and comments;

Mr. Donald Thompson and Mr. Ralph Wilson, Research Assistants, 1972–73, for much help in preparing the manuscript for the publisher, and Mrs. Joan Mohr for meticulous typing of the footnotes and index.

Berkeley, December, 1972

---

[1] Some support for this judgment may be offered by referring to a recent work on comparative law and legal studies. The bibliography, limited to English-language journal articles published between 1929 and 1969, lists almost 3,500 titles. Of these, at least 500 are about comparative law, or are comparative studies of some aspect of the law in two or more societies. Rudolf B. Schlesinger, *Comparative Law: Cases—Texts—Materials*, 3d ed. (Mineola, N.Y.: Foundation Pr. 1970), pp. 643–816.

1

Introduction

Concern and accomplishment on the international level have a long and honorable history in the librarianship of several Western countries, dating back, in some instances, over a century.

The Universities of Marburg and Breslau founded an *Akademischer Tauschverein* in 1817, chiefly for the purpose of the regular exchange of published dissertations. Additional German universities soon joined, and before mid-century, institutions in a number of other European countries were participating.

The Smithsonian Institution, Washington, D.C., founded in 1846, began in 1852 to send official government publications on international exchange, and began, also, the free shipment of publications of libraries and other institutions of the United States to their counterparts in other countries.

The founding meetings of the American Library Association (ALA), in 1876, and the (British) Library Association, a year later, were attended by librarians from Great Britain and the United States, respectively. The British meeting was also attended by representatives from Belgium, Denmark, France, and Italy.

A first international or world congress of librarians was held in Chicago, in 1893, in connection with the Columbian Exposition of that year, with librarians from England, France, and Germany in attendance. Additional international congresses were held in London in 1897, in St. Louis in 1904, in Brussels in 1910, in Paris in 1923, in Prague in 1926, and there have been others since. International interlibrary loan has already celebrated its diamond jubilee.

As early as 1900 the ALA had a committee on international cooperation that was succeeded in 1942 by the International Relations Board, which in turn, in 1956, became the International Relations Committee. An International Relations Office was begun in 1943 and had a paid staff in both Chicago and Washington until 1972. In the ALA there is also an International Relations Round Table that provides a forum and focus for some 600 librarians having international interests.

The International Federation of Library Associations (IFLA), founded in 1928, now (1973) has nearly 100 national library associations and 350 institutions in some 70 countries as members. The *Proceedings* (1931–68) of its annual meetings, now published in *IFLA Annual* . . . , reveal a great deal of attention to various aspects of international librarianship—national and university libraries, statistics, cataloging, interlibrary loan, and so on.

During the past quarter of a century, nearly one hundred internationally oriented conferences, institutes, and seminars have been held in almost as many countries.

Finally, scarcely any reader of these pages needs to be reminded of the large number of bibliographical and related works, such as the *World List of Scientific Periodicals, 1900–1921*, that have been produced with, and could not have been produced without, international cooperative effort.

Activity and interest in international affairs increased enormously in librarianship, as in many other fields, after the Second World War. This increase was the result of such developments as the creation of dozens of newly independent countries with their need for advice and aid in the development of modern libraries; international travel and study opportunities provided by such agencies as the Fulbright Commission, Smith-Mundt, the United States Department of State's Agency for International Development and its predecessors, the Organization of American States, the *Bibliothekarische Auslandsstelle* of the Federal Republic of Germany, the Council on Library Resources, Carnegie Corporation of New York, the Asia, Ford, Gulbenkian, Kellogg, and Rockefeller Foundations (some of which were active in international librarianship before World War II), and, especially, UNESCO, through its Division of Development of Documentation, Libraries, and Archives Services. Perhaps not least was the development of the transoceanic jet airplane.

With very few exceptions, the efforts of all of the named agencies, and others that might be mentioned, have been directed toward aiding individuals, specific institutions, countries, and regions (e.g., South-East Asia, South America), or toward attempting to provide solutions for library problems. Aside from a few undertakings, such as the International Conference on Cataloguing Principles of 1961, and the subsequent developments and accomplishments to which the conference led, international library activity has not had genuine comparative concerns or achievements—that is, there has been little or no effort devoted to the systematic gathering, examination, and synthesis of library data of any kind from two or more countries, societies, or cultures, in an effort to identify differences and similarities and arrive at explanations which account for the observed phenomena. This is not in any sense whatever to denigrate the very real and important accomplishments of librarianship on the international level. The many agencies and individuals responsible for these accomplishments had other and wholly legitimate ends in view, and librarianship almost everywhere has enormously benefited as a result. It is a contention of this essay, however, that librarianship is sadly deficient in the area of genuine comparative study. This question is considered in some detail in chapter 4.

At the same time there is substantial hard evidence to suggest a greatly increased interest in the general subject of comparative librarianship in recent years. In its first two quinquennial indices, 1950–55 and 1956–60, *Library Science Abstracts* (since 1969, *Library and Information Science Abstracts*) gives one entry each under the rubric, "Librarianship, comparative;" in the index for 1961–65, forty-six entries are given, and from 1966 to 1970, there were fifty-nine items. Our principal index of professional writing, *Library Literature*, had no separate heading for comparative librarianship until August 1971; up to that date, all relevant publications were entered under the heading "Librarianship—International Aspects."

The first year, 1963, in which the programs of American (and Canadian) library schools were broken down by fields and specializations covered, five schools—California, Berkeley; California, Los Angeles; Chicago; Columbia; and Wisconsin—were listed as offering work in comparative librarianship.[1] The corresponding figure today is forty-five.[2]

Some British library schools began inaugurating courses in the subject in 1966, and they now exist at the College of Librarianship, Aberystwyth, Wales; the Leeds Polytechnic; the Polytechnic of North London; the University of London; and the University of Sheffield. Other schools have plans under way. The schools in Copenhagen and Ibadan, among others, also pay some attention to the subject.

The increased interest in Great Britain is further exemplified by the formation, in 1968, of the "International and Comparative Librarianship Group" of the (British) Library Association and its quarterly publication, *Focus*. The Library Association

[1] *Journal of Education for Librarianship* 4:83–102, 107 (Fall 1963).

[2] Ibid., special ed. (1972), p. 105.

now includes "a paper," B 37, International and Comparative Librarianship, in its two-year course syllabus.

The very considerable increase, particularly since World War II, in publications, international study tours, international exchanges of personnel, surveys, conferences, institutes, and even library education programs, does not, unfortunately, suggest a great general interest in the field *as an area of serious study.* It is noteworthy that one of our leading journals could not so long ago publish an entire, monograph-length issue on research methods in librarianship without once mentioning either comparative method or comparative librarianship.[3]

What is being done in the library schools is either at an elementary level, practically oriented, and based upon more or less superficial observation rather than upon intensive investigation and solid research; or it is highly limited in scope; or it is unsupported either by research funds and staff or by adequate library facilities; or it is being done by over-burdened personnel for whom the area is but a small fraction of their total commitment. At a majority of institutions, more than one of these deterrents is present. This matter is considered further in chapter 4.

Comparative librarianship, or what passes for it outside of the formal library education programs, has been chiefly motivated by simple curiosity about foreign lands and their library practices; by a desire to aid developing areas—often by introducing in them techniques and practices in use in the surveyor's or consultant's own country; by a desire to borrow or adapt a foreign practice; by a felt need to solve a practical library problem; or by the hope of fostering international goodwill, cooperation, and brotherhood. All of these motives are laudable, and the achievements which have resulted from them have, without any doubt whatever, been beneficial to librarianship. But these motives are inadequate as bases either to justify or to sustain a solid field of study, and the results they have produced have seldom been either comparative or at an intellectually high level.

[3] *Library Trends* 13 (July 1964).

Comparative studies have achieved a valued position in the teaching and research programs of many disciplines. While the situation naturally varies considerably from field to field, the beginning of scholarly work in the majority lies in the nineteenth century, if not earlier; the contribution of such studies to the advancement of the discipline has been impressive and significant, and a substantial literature of both theory and practice has been created. A brief look at a few representative fields is illustrative and instructive. Before undertaking such a survey, it may be useful to note that the philosophical fathers were primarily Comte (1798–1857), Spencer (1820–1903), and John Stuart Mill (1806–73).

Comte saw a particular need to apply scientific principles to the study of society and sought scientifically to reconcile order and progress. He wanted a scientific history devoted to the discovery of laws which regulate social development. His approach was historical but, as he viewed social groups as living organisms, he believed that sociology could use a methodology similar to that of biology; in other words, a methodology of observation, experimentation, and comparison. The last, he thought, involved a rational comparison of the different states of human society. He viewed cultural differences, which he recognized as existing between different societies, as resulting from exceptional racial, climatic, and political factors. The comparative method for Comte involved, to oversimplify greatly, the development of a scientific history which would make possible discovery of the laws which regulate social development. Such a history, Comte believed, could be created by a comparative study of people and their cultures.

Spencer, also, wanted to make sociology a real science of society. The only history of practical value, he maintained, is descriptive sociology, which would narrate the lives of national societies to furnish material for a comparative sociology and for a subsequent determination of the ultimate laws to which social phenomena conform. Although the natural history of society

6

will not produce an exactly quantitative science like geology or biology, nevertheless, society being, in his view, an organism, biological laws could be applied to its study. He equated change with biological growth and drew general conclusions from the use of the comparative method. The theory of change in Spencer's law of evaluation is an essential part of the comparative method.

Although Mill did not himself use the comparative method, he did introduce Comte to English scholars, and Mill's *System of Logic* was intended to lay the logical basis for a science of society. The major problem, according to Mill, was to determine (1) the causes which produced and the phenomena which characterized the state of society generally, and (2) the laws according to which any state of society produces the state which succeeds it and takes its place. Mill thought social change resulted in progress and believed that the comparative method could be used to convert his philosophy of history into a science. The facts of history could then be studied comparatively to show how any state of society produces its successor.

Although the comparative method of Comte, Spencer, and Mill was not so much a method of inquiry as it was a preferred solution to a problem, these authors gave a reasoned, forceful, summary expression to the nineteenth century climate of opinion, and their advocacies were supported and fortified by the Darwinian hypothesis describing the mechanism of change in biological forms.

One of the earliest disciplines to evince an interest in the comparative was linguistics; in the fifteenth and sixteenth centuries, the rising importance of vernacular languages produced bi- or tri-lingual grammars and dictionaries. However, scientific linguistics is generally said to have begun with a speech given by Sir William Jones to the Asiatic Society of Bengal in 1785, thus antedating Comte, Spencer, and Mill. Jones, Chief Justice in Bengal, knew Hindustani and, in his speech, declared that Sanskrit bore to Latin, Greek, and Germanic "a stronger affinity,

7

both in the roots of verbs, and in the forms of grammar, than could possibly have been produced by accident; so strong, indeed, that no philologer could examine them all three without believing them to have sprung from some common source, which, perhaps, no longer exists." Jones's speech set off an explosion in European scholarship and eventually led to the production of countless comparative grammars of sub-family after sub-family of Indo-European and some non-Indo-European languages, as well as to a vastly increased understanding of the relationships and development of large numbers of languages. Friedrich von Schlegel, in his *Über die Sprache und Weisheit der Indier* (1808), used the term *vergleichende Grammatik* and maintained that a comparative study of Sanskrit and other languages would result in the same kind of information on the family relationship of languages that comparative anatomy had produced in biological science. A few years later, Rasmus Rask, a Dane, professor (and later librarian) at the University of Copenhagen, published the first "comparative grammar," a work which foreshadowed most of the methods and discoveries of the next half century and established in general terms the principles of his earlier *Investigation of the Origin of Old Norse or Icelandic* (1818), which set forth a full classification of the Indo-European languages. A year after Rask's volume, there appeared the first edition of *Deutsche Grammatik*, a milestone work by Jakob Ludwig Karl Grimm—the fairytale Grimm—which demonstrated how the Germanic languages could be descended from a common ancestor and still show the striking differences of form from Latin and Greek which they often did.

This work, laying out as it did, for the first time and in a rigorously scientific way, a grammar for all of the Germanic languages, and treating language as a constantly changing and growing living thing, indissolubly bound up with the life of the people, was revolutionary. In the first volume of a revised edition (1822), the author set out "Grimm's Law" regarding the pattern of consonantal changes in the Indo-European languages.

8

Another major work, in the field of comparative morphology rather than phonology, was Franz Bopp's *Über das Conjugationssystem der Sanskritsprache* . . . (1816). The next half century produced hundreds of studies, of which Grimm's work may fairly be said to be the original inspiration, first of Indo-European and often dead languages, later of non-Indo-European and living ones — such as Bantu, American Indian, and Malayo-Polynesian. One of those who pioneered the study of living languages was Wilhelm v. Humboldt who, in his *Über die Kawi-sprache* . . . (3 vols., 1836–39), attempted a scientific classification of non-Indo-European languages.

In a later work, *Vergleichende Grammatik* . . . (1833–70), Bopp, then professor at the University of Berlin, produced a comparative grammar of several Indo-European languages, and, at the end of the century, professors Karl Brugmann (Leipzig) and Berthold Delbrück (Jena), in *Grundriss der Vergleichenden Grammatik der Indo-germanischen Sprachen* (3d ed., 1897–1916), codified most of the major work which had been done earlier. New codifications have been provided by, among others, Jerzy Kurylowicz, in his *Indogermanische Grammatik* (1969).

The latter part of the century produced a number of major treatises on linguistic theory and studies, such as Max Müller's *Lectures on the Science of Language* . . . (1861–64) and William Dwight Whitney's *Language and the Study of Language* (1867) and *The Life and Growth of Language* (1875). Müller and Whitney were at the time professors at Oxford and Yale, respectively.

Whereas linguistic studies in the nineteenth century were generally more concerned with the taxonomic, the historical, and direct comparison between two or more languages, the interests of the twentieth century have shifted toward a more general and synchronic concern, and exacting, physical-science laboratory techniques have been employed for the determination of the sounds and relationships of different kinds of speech. Works of a philosophical/sociological kind, discussing the nature of

9

language itself and the difference between the language of a people and the speech of individuals, were increasingly common. Among such works was Ferdinand de Saussure's *Cours de Linguistique Générale* (1916). Important and valuable historical studies also continued to be produced, however, such as Antoine Meillet's *Introduction à l'Étude Comparative des Langues Indo-Européennes* (1903; 8th ed., 1937), and *Linguistique Historique et Linguistique Générale* (1921).

Some of the other principal high points of twentieth century linguistic study may be mentioned: Otto Jespersen's theoretical work on the development of language in general, *Language, Its Nature, Development, and Origin* (1922); Nikolai Trubetskoy's *Grundzüge der Phonologie* (1939), an attempt to interpret language sounds functionally in terms of sound patterns; Edward Sapir's *Language* (1921) and Leonard Bloomfield's work of the same title in 1933; Bernard Bloch's and George Trager's *Outline of Linguistic Analysis* (1942); J. Whatmough's *Language: A Modern Synthesis* (1956), Noam Chomsky's *Syntactic Structures* (1957); and Roman Jakobson's *Fundamentals of Language* (1956).

Through its studies, linguistics has achieved, not only for students of language itself, but for sociologists, anthropologists, and others, understanding of the relationship of languages to each other; of the development of individual languages and language in general; and of the nature of speech and its relation to language. In addition, it has produced, along with its descriptions and explanations, a large body of principles underlying the whole field.

It is not surprising that law was another field which early embraced and benefited from comparative study; that is, in this case, from the belief that the legal provisions and enactments of different countries or cultures could profitably be compared for the purpose of improving local law and of arriving at general principles. Aristotle, in fact, in his *Constitutions* and *Politics*, did something of this for the free Greek cities and, in the Middle Ages, theologians and other scholars engaged in the comparative observation of both secular and canon law.

As early as 1618, the great jurist, John Selden (1584–1654), in the preface to his *History of Tithes* . . . , stressed both the necessity and the importance of comparative studies, developed inevitably by the observation of national laws. In the *History*, he applied the principle of comparison, and this and his other works are sometimes said to mark the beginning of comparative legal history.

The first to write in advocacy of a science of comparative law appears to have been the German legal scholar, Anselm von Feuerbach who, in the preface to a work by Karl August Dominikus Unterholzner (1787–1838), *Juristische Abhandlungen* (1810), claimed that the major source of all discovery in political science is comparison; the observation of similarities and differences, and the reasons for both, are essential for real understanding. He relates his plea for a science of comparative law to the methods and achievements of linguistics.

The versatile Jakob Grimm who, among numerous other activities, was once a librarian and professor at the University of Göttingen, produced in his *Deutsche Rechtsalterthümer* (1828) a massive collection of comparative data on Germanic popular law, which not only related laws and legal traditions to each other, but also to local custom.

Another German legal scholar, Karl Josef Anton von Mittermaier (1787–1867), a follower of Feuerbach, based his numerous works, as for example, *Das Englische, Schottische und Nordamerikanische Strafverfahren* (1851), on comprehensive comparative material, English and American, as well as Continental.

Earlier than these last, and more important, probably, both for our interests here and for later developments, was Montesquieu's *De l'Esprit des Lois* (1748), in which, after describing the similarities and contrasts of the law in the major political jurisdictions of his day, he attempted to demonstrate how, or to

11

what extent, particular institutions were the result of forms of government, moral conditions, and even geographical factors. Even though *The Spirit of the Laws* is, by today's judgment, uncritical, incomplete, and, above all, primarily didactic in purpose, Montesquieu's ideas and methods influenced numerous later thinkers such as the great legal scholars Friedrich Savigny, of the University of Berlin, and Sir Henry Maine, professor at Cambridge and Oxford. The last-named, like many others in social fields, was stimulated by the advances in biological science, and especially by Darwinism, to apply scientific principles and methods to social facts and situations. In his *Ancient Law* (1861), Maine formulated a famous set of "laws" of universal sociological development from status to contract.

Interestingly enough, however, the more immediate stimulus for comparative jurisprudence was the epoch-making discoveries of philology, already referred to. Students of religion, anthropology, sociology, and folklore were also similarly incited; the relationships between the different branches of the Indo-European languages, demonstrated by the linguists, and their ability to show that the development of these languages proceeded on courses which might be studied in strictly scientific ways, in order to ascertain uniformities and principles, led workers in other fields to seek similar achievements through the same means.

In the United States, as it emerged from the Colonial period, lawyers turned to comparative law for the development of the American legal system, in part because of the inapplicability of existing English law. Foremost among those who did so were Judges James Kent and Joseph Story, both of whom were familiar with Continental law.

By the middle of the nineteenth century, comparative law in England received a strong impetus from the fact that the highest appellate court of the British Empire, the Privy Council, was obliged to adjudicate on matters involving a large number of foreign legal systems; it was consequently necessary that the legal profession in England have access to, and be familiar with, certain systems of foreign jurisprudence. A major work on comparative law resulting from this need was William Burge's *Commentaries on Colonial and Foreign Laws* . . . (1837). Later, toward the end of the century, the growing importance of private international law required both Continental and English scholars to resort to foreign law to an increasing extent. This is true today for large numbers of members of the legal profession in many countries.

Although comparative law was, up to about the middle of the nineteenth century, still in embryo, and its study was undertaken almost exclusively for the practical purpose of improving the legal system of a particular country, it did develop a method of careful and comprehensive empirical observation, and it did genuinely "compare."

Further, the year 1829 had already seen the founding of the *Kritische Zeitschrift für Rechtswissenschaft und Gesetzgebung des Auslandes*, concerned with the encouragement of the study of foreign law, and in 1832 and 1846, respectively, there were founded the Chair of Comparative Law at the Collège de France and the Chair of Comparative Criminal Law at the University of Paris. Many other similar chairs have, of course, been founded elsewhere since.

By 1869, the *Société de Législation Comparée* and its *Bulletin* had been founded in Paris, followed in 1872 by the Society's *Annuaire de Législation Étrangère*. The *Institut de Droit International* followed in 1873 and the English Society of Comparative Legislation in 1898. *Die Zeitschrift für Vergleichende Rechtswissenschaft* began in 1878. A first International Congress of Comparative Law was held in Paris in 1900.

The last half of the nineteenth century also witnessed the beginning of a veritable flood of serious studies. Rudolf von Jhering, in his *Vorgeschichte der Indoeuropäer* (1894), attempted to establish principles of Aryan public and private law. Jhering's

13

German compatriot, B. W. Leist, in several works, especially his *Alt-arisches Jus Civile* (1892–96), not merely formulated basic rules of Aryan law, but went on to trace their influence in the later development of law, demonstrating that some of the most fundamental legal concepts are of exceedingly early origin.

L. H. Morgan's "Systems of Consanguinity" (1869); A. H. Post's *Aufgaben einer Allgemeinen Rechtswissenschaft* (1891), *Die Anfänge des Staats- und Rechtslebens* (1878), and *Studien zur Entwicklungsgeschichte des Familienrechts* (1889); J. F. McLennan's *Patriarchal Theory* (1885); and R. Hildebrand's *Recht und Sitte auf den Verschiedenen Wirtschaftlichen Kulturstufen* (1896) are a minute sample of the hundreds of works in comparative jurisprudence produced by the end of the nineteenth century.

A motivating force in the growth of interest in comparative legal studies during the earlier years of this century, and a force of some relevant concern to librarianship, involved what might be called a change of attitude toward the general question of the value of comparative study. This change arose from a recognition of the dangers inherent in a policy of legal isolationism. This kind of isolation seems to be endemic in library education programs and is considered in detail in chapter 4.

An important development, no doubt in part related to the foregoing, was the creation in numerous countries, France, Great Britain, Germany, the Netherlands, and Sweden, among others, of comparative law institutes, usually university associated. These institutes are continuously engaged in comparative research, both as an academic pursuit and for the courts, and they have exerted a very considerable influence on the development of national law in many fields. An International Academy of Comparative Law was founded at The Hague in 1924.

It is unnecessary to describe the numerous specific contributions that comparative legal studies in this century have made to the understanding of the law and the improvement of legal practice almost everywhere. What is evident from even the most cursory review is that the law in most of the major countries of the world has developed a large body of comparative research, a substantial group of journals, an enormous monographic literature, and high-level departments, subdepartments, or chairs at many leading universities.

More than a score of journals, chiefly in English, French, German, Italian, and Spanish, have been established. Among these are the *International and Comparative Law Quarterly* (1952), a continuation of the *Journal of Comparative Legislation* (1896–1951); *American Journal of Comparative Law* (1952); *Revue Internationale de Droit Comparé* (1949), a continuation of the *Bulletin de la Société de Législation Comparée* (1869–1948); *Zeitschrift für Vergleichende Rechtswissenschaft* (1878); *Zeitschrift für Rechtsvergleichung* (1960); *Revista del Instituto de Derecho Comparado* (1953); and *Annuario di Diritto Comparato e di Studi Legislativi* (1927).

The field most nearly akin to librarianship is education. Like librarianship, education is concerned with institutions in a physical sense (schools, colleges, universities) and the political or institutional jurisdictions that support them; with administrative matters of all kinds, including especially personnel and finance; with books and reading; and, above all, with service to society. Of no other field that has achieved a prominent position in comparative studies can the same be said. It should at least be helpful, and may be instructive, to look somewhat more closely at the development and achievements of comparative studies in education.

The direct antecedents, at least, go back two centuries and more.[4] Johann Gottfried Herder's *Journal Meiner Reise im Jahre 1769* must be counted by almost any definition a work on com-

---

[4] For an excellent summary of the history of comparative and international education from classical times through the nineteenth century, see Stewart E. Fraser and William W. Brickman, eds., *A History of International and Comparative Education* (Glenview, Ill.: Scott, Foresman, c1968), pp. 1–19.

15

parative pedagogy, since his theory of pedagogical acculturation is primarily based on comparative description and analysis. Johann Peter Brinkmann's *Vergleichung der Erziehung der Alten mit der Heutigen und Untersuchung, welche von Beyden mit der Natur am meisten Übereinstimmt* (1784) may also fairly be described as a comparative study. More significant for the development of the field was *De Re Scholastica Anglica cum Germanica Comparata* (1795–98), generally held to be the first attempt to analyze simultaneously two contemporary school systems. Friedrich August Hecht, the author, arrived at what he considered the essential similarities and differences between the two systems.

This is perhaps enough to lead us into the nineteenth century and to the work of Marc-Antoine Jullien de Paris, *L'Esquisse et Vues Préliminaires d'un Ouvrage sur l'Éducation Comparée* (1817), in which the author specifically formulated both the purpose and methods of comparative studies in education. A few years later came John Griscom's *A Year in Europe . . .* (2 vols., 1823) in which he discusses in an open-minded manner his observations of educational institutions in France, Great Britain, Holland, Italy, and Switzerland. This work stands at about the beginning of the development of comparative education in the United States, though the report itself is not in any real sense comparative.

In 1832, the French philosopher and educator, Victor Cousin, published his historic *Rapport sur l'État de l'Instruction Publique dans Quelques Pays de l'Allemagne et Particulièrement en Prusse*. This was not actually a comparative study, but one which, in the English translation of the part on Prussia, *Report on the State of Public Instruction in Prussia* (1835), had such a marked effect on educational thinking in the United States that a number of leaders in the field, among them Horace Mann, were prepared to take over, with few modifications, the entire Prussian system. Two years later, in his *Report on Elementary Public Instruction in Europe*, Calvin Stowe, once librarian at

16

Bowdoin College, recommended to the Ohio legislature that the state adopt the Prussian system. The following year, 1838, Friedrich Thiersch, professor at the University of Munich, published an important German counterpart to Cousin's report, *Über den Gegenwärtigen Zustand des Öffentlichen Unterrichts in den Westlichen Staaten von Deutschland, in Holland, Frankreich und Belgien (On the Present Condition of Public Instruction in the Western States of Germany, in Holland, France, and Belgium)*. This report was the result of government-sponsored study trips, undertaken for the specific purpose of gaining, through a comparison of foreign schools with German ones, a clear insight into the strengths and weaknesses of the latter.

The work of Griscom, Cousin, Stowe, Thiersch, and others of the time, although almost exclusively descriptive, utilitarian, and didactic, aroused great interest in "foreign" educational systems and paved the way for later comparative work.

An early inquiry into the economics of education, and one of the earliest studies in which statistical comparisons were used, was Friedrich Harkort's *Remarks on the Prussian Primary School and Its Teachers* (1842). The study was based upon visits to schools in France and Prussia and used extensive statistical, especially economic, comparisons to support a series of recommended educational reforms.

Lorenz von Stein, professor at the University of Vienna, chiefly known as a jurist, sociologist, and founder of the science of public administration, addressed himself also to school administration in his major work, *Die Verwaltungslehre* (1865–68). The fifth and sixth parts of this work are concerned with school administration and in them von Stein stressed, among other things, the importance of the study of the organization and administration of the educational system, and recognized clearly that scientific investigation of it was essential.

Horace Mann in his "Seventh Report" (1844), as first secretary of the Massachusetts Board of Education, compared secondary education in England, Scotland, Ireland, France, Germany, and Holland. Mann's work was one of the first to consider cultural, political, and social backgrounds and to attempt assessment of educational values. Although almost exclusively concerned with the areas of school organization and methods of instruction, the work was truly pioneering.

The significance of this effort lies not in the fact that Mann was notably less purely descriptive, less utilitarian, less subjective, or less critical than his contemporaries, for he was not. Where he broke important new ground was in realizing that examination of a school system could be satisfactorily performed only by taking into account the economic, political, and social milieu in which the system exists. He further saw that the society of which the school system was a part was an evolutionary, dynamic one, the changes in which continuously influenced education.

Similarly pioneering in character were reports by Matthew Arnold, based upon visits to France and Germany in 1859 and 1865, on educational practices in those two countries, and his *Schools and Universities on the Continent* (1868).

Comparative analyses of different national systems of education were contained in Wilhelm Dilthey's *Ueber die Moeglichkeit einer Allgemeingueltigen paedagogischen Wissenschaft* (*Concerning the Possibility of a Universally Valid Science of Pedagogy*) (1888). Dilthey, a professor at the University of Berlin, believed that the central point of comparison should be the capacities that are the goals of education, and that a critical evaluation of the education systems' relationship to the political and social system could and must be made. Like von Stein before him, Dilthey attempted to recognize the directions of development in the existing parts of the educational system, and from there, to deduce norms for the practice of education.

A French contemporary of Dilthey's, Pierre Émile Levasseur, a statistician by training, held views not dissimilar to those of his German colleague. He, too, stressed the importance of cultural factors as a base for the explanation of educational variation, but, reflecting his professional background, he laid great emphasis on the importance of codified data and made systematic efforts to relate educational variation to cross-national forces. In a paper given at the International Institute of Statistics in Vienna, 1891, he surveyed in depth the educational history, finances, and administration of ten European countries and, through analysis of his data, ranked each country according to several educational criteria. Levasseur believed that every kind of social factor had a potential effect upon one or another aspect of the educational system, that the effect of every given factor might be neutralized by another, that no single factor operated wholly independently of others, and that all forces in society—including climate, race, religion, and politics—are related to each other and to educational development.[5]

Among other early studies, influential either for their effect upon practice, or their contributions to the development of the field, or both, were Ernst G. Fischer's *Über die Englischen Lehranstalten in Vergleichung mit den Unsrigen* (1827), and the five-volume *Reports on Technical Instruction* by the Royal Commissioners of Great Britain (1884).

The foregoing is a bare summary of a small sample of the many hundreds of comparative studies, particularly of schools, school systems, and instructional methods, produced during the nineteenth century. The overwhelming majority of these studies —the work of Dilthey and Levasseur being notable exceptions— wherever undertaken and published, had, like early comparative law, the wholly practical purpose of improving local systems and practices. That is, the aim was to see whether an examination of what was being done in another country or countries would reveal something which could be beneficially adopted in or adapted to the author's own country. In view of this aim, and in view of the early state of the art, it is not surprising that most of these studies were unsystematic and somewhat subjective,

[5] See his *La Statistique de l'Enseignement Primaire* (Rome: Imprimerie Nationale de J. Bertero, 1892).

19

that comparisons were not always entirely valid, and that the "scientific" methodology would be open to substantial criticism by the standards of today. Nonetheless, the way was paved for the development of a science of comparative education in the twentieth century.

Even to list, with little or no comment, the most important contributions of the past three-quarters of a century would be a task requiring a great deal of time and space. A few landmark contributions, however, may be noted by way of illustration.

The logical and chronological beginning is Sir Michael Sadler's "How Far Can We Learn Anything of Practical Value from the Study of Foreign Systems of Education?" published in 1900. In this essay, as well as in much of his work thereafter, particularly as Director of the Office of Special Inquiries and Reports at the Board of Education, London, Sadler constantly stressed the relationship between the school and other elements of society, and the value of comparative education. He went so far as to deny the validity of comparisons which were made exclusively on the basis of educational factors; on the contrary, a country's schools could be satisfactorily studied solely in the light of the historical and social forces which inevitably shaped them. Certainly much, and probably most of the work in comparative education during the first half of this century was influenced by Sadler. Although these views had been adumbrated by some earlier writers such as Matthew Arnold, Dilthey, Levasseur, and Horace Mann, they had never been so emphasized or so explicitly and forcefully stated; from then on they were to dominate.

Among the earliest studies which constituted serious attempts to set forth, in a scientific manner, fundamental principles of educational systems, were Charles H. Thurber's *The Principles of School Organization* . . . (1900). In this study, Thurber examined the organization of the school systems of England, France, Germany, and the United States, relating the situation in each country to national backgrounds and conditions. Thurber's significance, however, lies not so much in the substance of a good study as in the method and spirit which he consciously brought to it, and in his explicit recognition of the significance and value of genuinely comparative studies.

Abraham Flexner's three well-known works, *Medical Education in the United States and Canada* (1910), *Medical Education in Europe* (1912), and *Medical Education: A Comparative Study* (1925), like Thurber's study, examined educational problems in the context of their social and political backgrounds and sought to arrive at fundamental principles. The same may be said of Flexner's later, and equally well-known work, *Universities: American, English, German* (1930). Paul Monroe's *Essays in Comparative Education* (1927 and 1932), Peter Sandiford's (ed.) *Comparative Education: Studies of the Educational Systems of Six Modern Nations* (1918), and William Learned's *The Quality of the Educational Process in the United States and Europe* (1927), of about the same period, were also comparative studies in some sense of the phrase. Sergius Hessen, a Russian philosopher and educator, at the time professor at Prague, produced in 1928 what was apparently the first effort at dealing with the whole field of comparative education at the secondary level, from a philosophical point of view: "Kritische Vergleichung des Schulwesens der Anderen Kulturstaaten," which appeared as part of the *Handbuch der Pädagogik*. In this work, Hessen addressed himself to problems of educational policies in four areas: compulsory education; the school and the state; the school and the church; and the school and economic life. He analyzed what he considered the underlying principles governing modern educational legislation in numerous countries.

A few years later, one of the major figures in the field, Isaac L. Kandel, published his *Comparative Education* (1933), a classic work which became a text in many universities in England and the United States. Kandel devoted particular attention to nationalism and the national character as historical background to existing educational conditions. He thus, following Sadler, formulated the necessity of an historical approach and suggested that

21

comparative studies require "first an appreciation of the intangible, impalpable spiritual and cultural forces which underlie an educational system; the factors and forces outside the school matter even more than what goes on inside it."[6] Kandel's monographic study, "Comparative Education," published in 1936, in *Review of Educational Research*, expressed the same idea and explicitly stated the derivatory view that "the purpose of comparative education, as of comparative law, comparative literature, or comparative anatomy, is to discover the differences in the forces and causes that produce differences in educational systems" and to discover the underlying principles which govern the development of all national systems of education.[7] Kandel was also the first since Levasseur to stress the importance of a statistical approach. Professor Nicholas Hans of Kings College, University of London, in the *Yearbook of Education* (1936 and 1937) and in his *Comparative Education . . .* (1949), and Friedrich Schneider, at the time director of the *Institut für Vergleichende Erziehungswissenschaft* (Institute of Comparative Education), Salzburg, and editor of the *International Review of Education,* in his *Triebkräfte der Pädagogik der Völker* (1947), also adopted, and even further emphasized, the historical approach and the necessity of historical understanding as a basis for comparative studies.

A work by J. F. Cramer and G. S. Browne is illustrative of some of the foregoing. In their *Contemporary Education: A Comparative Study of National Systems*, the authors examine chiefly the school systems of Australia, Canada, England, France, the USSR, and the United States, by looking at the political, economic, linguistic, and other external factors which influence the nature and development of national educational systems. The authors then examine internal factors such as ad-

[6] Isaac L. Kandel, *Comparative Education* (New York: Houghton Mifflin, c1933), p. xix.

[7] Isaac L. Kandel, "Comparative Education," *Review of Educational Research* 6:406 (Oct. 1936).

ministration, finance, and organizational forms. Finally, the significance of the historical development of the program of study and of the educational philosophy accounting for differences in the several systems is presented.[8]

The basic view of these later works was, of course, a far cry from earlier studies which were chiefly concerned with discovering whether and how local practices might be improved. In general, it may be said that comparative education has followed somewhat the same pattern of development as that of other established comparative studies. It began with simple descriptions, followed by classification of existing phenomena, moved toward an attempt, through analysis and comparison, to look for common origins and differentiation through historical development, and from this position proceeded to an attempt to seek causes and formulate general principles underlying all differences and variations.

From 1924 to 1944 Kandel was editor of the *Educational Yearbook* of the International Institute of Teachers College, Columbia University. In this capacity he collected and published an enormous amount of information regarding the educational systems of most parts of the world. The updated and expanded version of his 1933 text, with the title *The New Era in Education: A Comparative Study* (1955) further developed and exemplified his views, and it remains a basic work in the field.

William W. Brickman, among numerous other contributions, including bibliographical ones, was largely responsible for the creation of the Comparative Education Society in 1956. The Comparative Education Society in Europe was founded in 1961. The field has now so developed that a World Congress of Comparative Education Societies could be held in Ottawa in 1970.

Along with its vast, indeed intimidating, monographic literature, comparative education has created, especially since World

---

[8] J. F. Cramer and G. S. Brown, *Contemporary Education: A Comparative Study of National Systems* (New York: Harcourt, Brace, c1956).

War II, over a score of journals more or less exclusively concerned with the field. Among those directly and specifically devoted to it may be mentioned *Comparative Education* (1964); *Comparative Education Review* (1957); *International Review of Education* (1955), produced by the UNESCO Institute for Education in Hamburg; *L'Actualité Pédagogique à L'Étrangère* (1965); *Oversea Education* (1929); *International Association of Universities Bulletin* (1953); *Revista di Legislazione Scolastica Comparata* (1955); *The International Journal of Adult and Youth Education* (1961); and *Vergleichende Pädagogik* (1965).

Comparative education became a part of the academic curriculum, at least at some American universities, by the beginning of this century. At present, about thirty institutions have developed the field to the extent of having a particular department, or subdepartment, and a full-time faculty. Centers also exist in major universities elsewhere, not only in Europe—especially Belgium, France, Germany, Great Britain, Italy, the Netherlands, Switzerland, and the USSR—but also in Argentina, Brazil, Canada, Colombia, India, and Japan, among other countries.

The development of comparative education has been substantially furthered, and workers in the field have been supported and aided, by the specific concern and activity of a number of governments and non-governmental agencies, including those of France, with its *Institut Pédagogique National;* Germany, with a documentation and information center in Bonn; UNESCO, with the International Bureau of Education, Geneva, and the Institute for Education, University of Hamburg; the Netherlands, with its Central Statistical Bureau at The Hague; the USSR, with a branch for the Study of Pedagogy Abroad of the Institute of Theory and History of the Academy of Pedagogical Sciences; and the United States, among others.

In the United States, the Office of Education began research in comparative studies as long ago as 1868. The Office's International Educational Relations Branch maintains full-time specialists for all areas of the world, has developed a major library and statistical resource, and issues, among other publications, a *Bulletin* and *Studies in Comparative Education.*

It should probably be noted that comparative education is not without its severe and vocal critics, both among educators in general and among those within the area itself. Critics claim that most of the literature is thin, and largely descriptive; that factual and narrative works greatly outnumber the carefully explanatory and the rigorously scientific; that generally accepted criteria for evaluation are largely lacking; that a consistent and defensible methodology has not been developed; and that a priori judgments and personal biases characterize much of what has been produced.[9] This is not the place to pass judgment upon, or evaluate, these and other criticisms, even if the writer were equipped to do so. However great their validity, it is still indisputably a fact, as later chapters in this essay attempt to demonstrate, that comparative librarianship has not even begun to approach the achievements and developments of comparative studies in education—or linguistics, anthropology, law, government, religion, or sociology.

While the results of comparative studies—like the results of most scholarly inquiry in general—are initially of concern chiefly to the specialist, even the layman, if he pauses to reflect, must be aware that his view and knowledge of the world about him have been broadened and enriched by the work of comparativists. The work of Sir James Frazer in religion and customs, particularly his *The Golden Bough;* James Bryce in politics, especially his *Modern Democracies;* and the contributions of Margaret Mead in anthropology, to mention just three Anglo-American writers in as many fields, are household concepts.

---

[9] For a vigorous statement on these points, see Harold J. Noah and Max A. Eckstein, *Toward a Science of Comparative Education* (New York: Macmillan, 1969), pp. 184–86. See also Robert G. Templeton, "Some Reflections on the Theory of Comparative Education," *Comparative Education Review* 2:27–31 (Oct. 1958).

It has been the intent of this brief introductory statement to suggest that:

1. Comparative studies in a number of fields have made marked and significant contributions to the development and understanding of the parent discipline, and to knowledge about it.

2. By inference, comparative studies in librarianship, if soundly developed, might be expected to have similar beneficial effects upon librarianship as a whole.

3. To the extent that comparative studies in other fields have achieved a genuinely scholarly status and made lasting contributions, they have done so through a vigorous application of scientific methods of inquiry.

4. The developments in other disciplines, whatever the nature of their beginnings, have moved always closer to the employment of scientific method, and toward a search for explanations, and for principles and "laws" which underlie observed phenomena and aid in understanding how or why the phenomena have come to be as they are.

2

The Dimensions of Terminology, Definition and Scope

It may be observed at the outset of this discussion that "comparative librarianship"—like "comparative education" and "comparative law"—is something of a misnomer. As discussed more fully in chapter 5, the matter dealt with in this study is not a sub-discipline or sub-field, like information science or bibliography, but rather, primarily a method and approach. To speak logically and exactly, therefore, we should use the phrase "comparative method in librarianship." But logic and exactitude have to yield here to custom and tradition; "comparative librarianship" is already so ingrained in the profession's thinking and literature—and established as a subject heading in *Library Literature* and *Library and Information Science Abstracts*—as to make change impossible now. "Comparative librarianship" has at least the virtue of brevity and, like "comparative education" and "comparative law," was perhaps first adopted for that reason.

It is an hypothesis of this essay that one of the deterrents to the advancement of comparative studies in librarianship is the great confusion which exists as to what comparative librarianship really is, and the conflicting, often internally self-contradictory views which have been expressed about it. We can hardly expect precision of product if there is imprecision in meaning and understanding, and if we have no generally accepted definitions and terminology.[1]

A review of what has been written on this point supports the minor premise of the hypothesis. The review is presented chronologically. Theoretically, one would expect that, as time

[1] It is worth remarking that the term "comparative librarianship," or "librarianship, comparative," is not included in any of the profession's standard dictionaries and glossaries. Thus, it is not found in L. M. Harrod's *The Librarians' Glossary* (London: Grafton, 1938 and 1959; London: Deutsch, 1971) or in American Library Assn., Committee on Library Terminology, A.L.A. *Glossary of Library Terms* (Chicago: The Association, 1943). S. Simsova's and M. MacKee's *A Handbook of Comparative Librarianship* (London: Bingley, c1970) is in error in citing (p. 14) a definition from Harrod's "new ed (Deutsch, 1969)"; there is, in fact, no 1969 edition of Harrod.

The concept "comparative librarianship" is also lacking from the following dictionaries and glossaries: Anthony Thompson et al., comp., *Vocabularium Bibliothecarii*, 2nd ed. (UNESCO, 1962); *Bibliotekstermer* (Lund: Bibliotekstjänst, 1965); Universitní Knihovna v Olomouci, *Slovník Knihovnických Termínů v Šesti Jazycích* (Prague: Státní Pedagogické Nakl, 1958); Zoltán Pipics, *Dictionarium Bibliothecarii Practicum* (Munich-Pullach: Verlag Dokumentation, 1971); Beatriz Massa de Gil et al., comp., *Technical Dictionary of Librarianship* (Mexico: Editorial F. Trillas, 1964); M. H. Saringulian, comp., *English Russian Dictionary of Library and Bibliographical Terms* (Moscow: All-Union Book Chamber, 1958); Otti Gross, *Library Terms* (Hamburg: Stichnote, 1952); Fujio Mamiya, comp., *A Complete Dictionary of Library Terms* (Tokyo: Japan Library Bureau, 1952); Japan, Ministry of Education, comp., *Japanese Scientific Terms: Library Science* (Tokyo: Tosho, 1958); Domingo Buonocore, *Diccionario de Bibliotecología* (Santa Fe: Castellví, 1963); Kosta Grubačić, *Enciklopedijski Leksikon Bibliotekarstva* (Sarajevo: Zavod za Izdavanje Udžbenika, 1964); Harold A. Mattice, "Lexicon of Bibliographical, Cataloguing and Library Terms in English, Chinese and Japanese," *Bulletin of the New York Public Library* 48: 451–70, 555–70 (May-June 1944).

went on, and as more people gave thought to the matter and could build upon the work of previous writers, we should find greater precision, greater uniformity, and greater agreement. This, unfortunately, is not the case. Some of the later statements and views are just as imprecise, just as conflicting, and just as internally self-contradictory as earlier ones.

1954a

One of the earliest opinions, expressed by Chase Dane, offers the view that comparative librarianship "is a study of library science in many countries to discover what factors are common to those countries and which are unique to one. It is an evaluation of the philosophies and policies of librarianship on an international scale to determine long-range trends, to appraise shortcomings, and to uncover contradictions and inconsistencies between practice and theory."[2] This is more a statement of purpose than of definition. Entirely omitted is any thought of what really constitutes "comparative," and any notion that comparative studies should seek to provide explanations and to discover principles. However, Dane's title, "The Benefits of Comparative Librarianship," does not promise a definition.

1954b

Almost simultaneously, Dane published a second article in which he offered a considerably expanded, and in one respect improved, definition of comparative librarianship:

> It is a study of library development in many countries to discover what developments have been successful and can be copied elsewhere. It is an examination of the philosophies and policies of librarianship on an international

[2] Chase Dane, "The Benefits of Comparative Librarianship," *The Australian Library Journal* 3:89 (July 1954).

scale to determine long-range trends, to appraise short-comings, and to uncover contradictions and inconsistencies between practice and theory. Above all it is the study of the cause and effect of library development throughout the world.[3]

Much of this definition, also, has to do with motivation, purpose, and value, but it does introduce, by implication at least, the notion of explanation of observed phenomena in the phrase "study of the cause and effect of library development throughout the world."

1958

In describing an introductory, but graduate-level seminar in comparative librarianship which she began in 1956 at the School of Library Service, Columbia University, Dorothy Collings writes that the seminar "provides comparative study of the library systems, problems and attempted solutions of various countries, considered within the context of the social, economic, political, and other factors prevailing in the area."

The aims of the seminar are:

1) To study available data concerning the library systems, problems, and solutions of selected countries, in the light of their particular circumstances;
2) To gain perspective on, and added insight into, the library problems which obtain in one's own situation;
3) To assist in the development of data and techniques for the comparative study of librarianship;
4) To assist in the advancement of international cooperation in the field of library development.[4]

[3] Chase Dane, "Comparative Librarianship," *The Librarian and Book World* 43:141 (Aug. 1954).

[4] Dorothy Collings, "Meeting the Needs of Foreign Students," *Library Journal* 83:3064 (Nov. 1, 1958).

This, too, is mostly concerned with aim and purpose; definition is implied rather than stated. Also, of course, the aims of a graduate seminar on a topic are not necessarily the same as those of the sub-discipline or study as a whole, and it would be unfair to assume that Collings intended her statement of aims to constitute a definition. She has given one, however, in her contribution described below under 1971.

1964

"Comparative librarianship," writes Carl M. White, "is a subject which deals with material on theory and practice found in different geographical and political areas, but it is a method of study as well as a subject."[5] This is not really a definition, and no doubt White did not intend it to be a precise one. However, it is all that he offers in his article. Again, nothing is said about what "comparative" really is or means.

1965a

D. J. Foskett suggests that "the beginning of the comparative method is the collection of data, the observation (as objectively as possible) of existing systems, and their measuring by means of some hypothetical or actual situation that we have set up as our point of reference," and that, in comparative studies, the past is studied "in order to discover patterns of progress in given social situations, for the purpose of measuring such patterns against other patterns, to see their similarities and their differences."[6] Again, hardly a real definition. See, however, his later, greatly expanded and developed article below (1965b).

[5] Carl M. White, "Comparative Study of Library Systems," in Carl M. White, ed., *Bases of Modern Librarianship* (Oxford: Pergamon Pr., 1964), p. 13.

[6] D. J. Foskett, "Comparative Librarianship," *The Library World* 66: 295–96 (June 1965).

31

1965b

"The beginning of comparative studies, then, is the collection of data; but we do not collect these data for their own sake. Case histories provide a great deal of data, but we are not concerned here with library history. What we are trying to do, in comparative studies, is to unravel the strands that go to make up a certain pattern, to assess these strands against those that make up other, different patterns, and to try to form estimates of the relative values of each. . . . Thus the objects of comparative studies cover the whole field of an activity."[7]

Although the quotations cited do not really constitute a definition, Foskett makes clear throughout his second article that comparative work implies cross-national, cross-cultural, or cross-geographical considerations; that it must be rooted in an understanding of the social forces which produced the library; and that it must be concerned with a search for causation.

1966a

Comparative librarianship, says Miles M. Jackson, is "that field of study that deals with the comparison of the theory and practice of librarianship in different countries. . . ."[8] The use in the definition of the word to be defined is seldom very helpful and "comparison of the theory and practices of librarianship in different countries" is too general to be of much help.

1966b

Louis Shores suggests that comparative librarianship is "the study and comparison of library theory and practice in all of

[7] D. J. Foskett, "Comparative Librarianship," in Robert L. Collison, ed., *Progress in Library Science, 1965* (London: Butterworths, 1965), pp. 126, 127.

[8] Miles M. Jackson, Jr., "Libraries Abroad," *The Journal of Library History* 1:133 (Apr. 1966).

the different countries of the world."[9] This definition, again, uses the concept to be defined in the definition and is too vaguely general to be of much assistance.

1968

"No practicing librarian," according to K. C. Harrison, "can afford to ignore comparative librarianship. It could be defined as being the comparative study of administrative practices throughout the developed library areas."[10] Aside from defects of omission in this statement, "comparative librarianship" can hardly be satisfactorily defined by the use of the phrase "comparative study," and no logical justification can be advanced for limiting its scope either to "administrative practices" or to "the developed library areas."

1969

An institute held at the University of Oklahoma School of Library Science in August 1969 adopted as a guide to its discussion the definition: "comparative librarianship consists of study of one or more aspects of library theory, practice or influence in two or more societies or geographical areas" and considered comparative librarianship "a sub-discipline of the general subject of international librarianship."[11]

1970a

Reference is made here to an article by Martin H. Sable and Lourdes Deya about a proposed course in international and

[9] Louis Shores, "Why Comparative Librarianship?" *Wilson Library Bulletin* 41:204 (Oct. 1966).

[10] K. C. Harrison, an oral statement, made at the (British) Library Association headquarters, quoted by Marigold L. Cleeve, "International and Comparative Librarianship 1967–1968," *International Library Review* 1:95 (Jan. 1969).

[11] H. C. Campbell, "Internationalism in U.S. Library School Curricula," *International Library Review* 2:184 (Apr. 1970).

comparative librarianship simply to note that the authors do not undertake to define either of these terms, but rather at times use them interchangeably.[12]

1970b

Shores, long a proponent of comparative librarianship, repeats verbatim his definition of comparative librarianship quoted in entry 1966b.[13] However, in the later rather sentimental and highly subjective piece, he offers a number of amplifying statements, of which the following are the most pertinent:

> Like the rest of the world, we librarians suffer from the same malady that has afflicted all mankind: a lack of significant comparisons. . . . But our profession and its discipline can never reach their high destiny until they begin to compare more significantly. Librarians the world over can never assume their decisive role until librarianship becomes comparative. . . . We must begin by comparing ourselves with each other, individually as librarians, collectively as libraries, in our own community, in our state, region, nation, world . . . *on equal footing.* This is the basic approach in all comparative study. It is the essence of Comparative Librarianship and its theoretical approach.[14]

> Comparative Librarianship offers a qualitative measure of our contemporary brand of intellectual freedom. . . .[15]

In discussing censorship, and suggesting a role for comparative

[12] Martin H. Sable and Lourdes Deya, "Outline of an Introductory Course in International and Comparative Librarianship," *International Library Review* 2:187–92 (Apr. 1970).

[13] Louis Shores, "Comparative Librarianship: A Theoretical Approach," in Miles M. Jackson, Jr., ed., *Comparative and International Librarianship* (Westport, Conn.: Greenwood, 1970), p. 5.

[14] Ibid., pp. 4–5.

[15] Ibid., p. 7.

librarianship, the author asks, with a complete change in the use of the substantive word:

> As we look at the contemporary library scene, are we comparatively free or comparatively censored?[16]

> It is Comparative Librarianship that must call us back to perspective on the current crusade for intellectual freedom. . . . Sophisticated reviewers may feel free to express uncritical admiration of sheer "frankness," but Librarianship, especially if it is comparative, must not abdicate its literary judgment, no matter how celebrated the name of the reviewer who extolls the book under consideration.[17]

> If libraries could anticipate issues that stimulate violence, lure potential marchers off the streets and into reading rooms to document problems, and identify solutions so superior that their adoption would irresistibly overcome current social evils, then Comparative Librarianship would be approaching its own high role.[18]

> Of course, the symbol of all Comparative Librarianship is comparison with librarianship abroad.[19]

En passant, in view of this last categorical statement, one is at a loss to understand how Shores can justify the title of another article, "Public Library U.S.A.: An Essay in Comparative Librarianship," the content of which is wholly devoted to the United States.[20]

> Part of our professional complex is to underestimate our discipline, our education, our research and, above all, our

[16] Ibid., pp. 8–9.
[17] Ibid., pp. 9–10.
[18] Ibid., p. 13.
[19] Ibid., p. 19.
[20] Louis Shores, "Public Library U.S.A.: An Essay in Comparative Librarianship," in Robert F. Vollans, ed., Libraries for the People: International Studies in Librarianship, in Honour of Lionel R. McColvin, C.B.E., F.L.A. (London: Library Assn., 1968), pp. 239–56.

professional literature and our professional philosophy. We do so, partially, because of our diffident, tip toe, whispering vocational climate. But we do so even more because we lack comparisons. If we compare ourselves with some of the other disciplines, even the ones that have retained their prestige longest in the history of scholarship, we will be convinced that the art, if not the science, on which our vocation is based has an equal claim with philosophy to the definition "the sum of all knowledge." Another look, comparatively, at all education of the past and the present, general and special, will establish our library education as not only peer but as containing some fundamental elements for all learning.[21]

Librarianship needs not only to make comparisons but qualitative ones especially.[22]

There is much more in similar vein, suggesting moralistic and welfare aims and values which are quite out of place even if it were made clear, as it is not, how and through what methods the desired results would be achieved.

1970c

In the same year, Shores published another paper in which he again repeats the definition quoted in entry 1966b. He then adds, "an amplification of this definition that has been implied, but not adequately stressed, is that comparisons within a country may be just as significant as comparisons with other countries."[23] As discussed in detail later in this chapter, this inclusion, referring as it does to comparisons "within a country," runs completely counter to accepted definitions of comparative studies today in the social sciences, including education.

[21] Shores, "Comparative Librarianship," p. 20.

[22] Ibid., p. 22.

[23] Louis Shores, "Librarian, Know Yourself," *Canadian Library Journal* 27:451 (Nov.-Dec., 1970).

1970d

In the first thirty-six pages of text proper of a monograph on comparative librarianship, Sylvia Simsova wrestles with problems of terminology and definition and attempts to reconcile the views of earlier writers.[24] The author begins by quoting the definitions provided by Dane, Foskett, Harrod, Jackson, Shores, and White, discussed above.[25] She then suggests that "Each of these definitions gives varying degrees of emphasis to three main points. Firstly, the practical usefulness of comparative librarianship as a tool for cultural borrowing. . . . Secondly, the comparative method as a tool for bringing order into material (and thinking) about librarianship. . . . Lastly, an element of internationalism, hinted at by Dane, expressed by Jackson and rather overemphasized by Shores."[26]

Neither of the first two points Simsova makes is a definitional one; the first relates to value and benefit, the second to methodology and value. Simsova's third point introduces the word "internationalism." She continues by suggesting that "An examination of the term 'comparative librarianship' would probably reveal that the meaning given to it least frequently is the one expressed by Foskett, and yet it is the one to which the word 'comparative' is most appropriate. In the other two meanings it could be replaced by 'international' without distorting the definition to any great extent. What is the difference between 'international librarianship' and 'comparative librarianship'? These terms are usually applied to a variety of activities without any attempt at defining them; sometimes, as in the name given to the International and Comparative Librarianship Group of the Library Association, they are used jointly to make sure that nothing is left out."[27]

[24] Simsova and MacKee, *Handbook*, esp. pp. 14–17 and 25–27.

[25] As pointed out in the first footnote to this chapter, the citation to Harrod is a "ghost."

[26] Simsova and MacKee, *Handbook*, p. 15.

[27] Ibid., p. 16.

Simsova then lists five activities "known under the umbrella terms 'comparative and international librarianship'," defining the fourth, international activities, as "cooperation, assistance to developing countries, international understanding," and the fifth as "development of comparative librarianship as a subject, methodology." The author then destroys this distinction by saying that, if "comparative librarianship is primarily an academic discipline using the comparative method . . . , it is possible to say that any of the above activities can be described by the name 'comparative,' provided they are carried out as an academic discipline and provided they use methods of systematic inquiry. If this is not the case they should be described by the term 'international.' Thus it can be said that a study tour of libraries which aims at promoting international understanding comes under the heading 'international,' but another study tour planned to compare the solution of a particular problem in a number of countries should come under the heading of 'comparative'."[28]

And then: "In defining 'comparative' librarianship, it is useful to remember that in many other sciences the term 'comparative' is not synonymous with 'international.' The geographical element has been introduced into comparative sciences by the social sciences, such as anthropology, and has no place in comparative natural sciences such as comparative anatomy and others." After then citing a definition of comparative anatomy as a "comparison of the whole body with all its most remarkable parts, that is, the mutual relationship of the whole and its parts," she suggests that this definition "applied to comparative librarianship extends . . . the definition to studies that do not necessarily cross national boundaries, e.g., a comparison of rural and municipal library services within the same country." This is at best misleading and at worst self-contradictory, since librarianship is clearly not a "natural science."[29]

28 Ibid., p. 16.
29 Ibid., pp. 16–17.

Simsova's distinction between "comparative" and "international" is a very imprecise one, and to suggest that studies are "comparative" or not, depending upon whether they are "carried out as an academic discipline," is absurd. A few, at least, of the best comparative studies in librarianship, as in other disciplines, have been conducted outside of any academic connection whatever.

Later, in a section on the types of comparative studies, Simsova writes, "The various viewpoints of comparative studies can be illustrated by a selection of works related to American librarianship," following which she cites a number of publications that are comparative in nature or, at least, have comparative elements. She then says, "Finally, here are two examples of American views of American libraries: A E Bostwick *The American public library* (Appleton, 1929), R D Leigh *The public library in the United States: the general report of the Public Library Inquiry* (Columbia Univ. p, 1950)."[30] Neither of these two works is in the slightest degree comparative.

In sum, Simsova does not herself offer a definition of comparative librarianship, she does not usefully analyze or reconcile the several definitions she quotes and, where she offers terminological distinctions, she is often imprecise, misleading, or self-contradictory.

1971

The most precise and, considering its source (*Encyclopedia of Library and Information Science*), presumably the most "authoritative" statement runs:

> Comparative librarianship may be defined as the systematic analysis of library development, practices, or problems as they occur under different circumstances (most usually in different countries), considered in the context

[30] Ibid., pp. 27–28. Punctuation and capitalization as in the original.

of the relevant historical, geographic, political, economic, social, cultural, and other determinant background factors found in the situations under study. Essentially, it constitutes an important approach to the search for cause and effect in library development, and to the understanding of library problems.

Comparative librarianship frequently uses historical data, but it differs from library history in that it is concerned primarily with providing a clearer view of current library problems and the process of library development.

Comparative librarianship is also closely related to efforts aimed at international understanding and cooperation in librarianship, but its lively concern with and usefulness to these activities grows out of its basic preoccupation with the systematic search for accurate understanding and interpreting of library practices and results in differing cultural contexts. . . .

As stated above, the basic purpose of comparative librarianship as a subject of scholarly concern is to seek full understanding and correct interpretation of the library system or problem under review.[31]

Aside from the fact that the primary concern of comparative librarianship is not to provide "a clearer view of current library problems," and that the phrase, "most usually in different countries," does not go far enough, this definition by Dorothy Collings is quite satisfactory. But then, having strongly implied the presence of a cross-national, or cross-cultural element, the author, in a later discussion of the major types of comparative librarianship studies, speaks of:

(1) *Area studies*, which provide a descriptive survey and critical analysis of library development in a given country or region, in the context of relevant determinant background factors;

[31] Dorothy G. Collings, "Comparative Librarianship," *Encyclopedia of Library and Information Science*, 5:492–93 (New York: Marcel Dekker, 1971).

(2) *Cross-national* or *cross-cultural studies of* . . . (b) A technical library problem as dealt with in two or more countries (or *different situations in the same country*) [emphasis added] . . . ; and

(3) *Case studies*, which provide analysis in depth of a type of library or a key factor in library development, such as library education, literacy, or book production, *in a particular country* [emphasis added].[32]

It may be noted here, first, that a study of "different situations in the same country" cannot be a "cross-national" study; and second, that the entire concept of comparative studies is violated on the points of logic, common sense, dictionary definitions, and the findings, experience, and development of other disciplines, when we include within their sphere, and accept as such, books or projects limited to a specific country or cultural milieu. Those who would maintain otherwise must be required to defend their position. Neither "a descriptive survey and a critical analysis of library development" in, for example, the Netherlands, nor the study of a "technical library problem," such as classification, automation, or book selection in Israel, nor an "analysis . . . of . . . library education" in West Germany is a comparative study, any more than would be the study of the elementary schools of Massachusetts. The anthropologist may study as deeply and as intensively as he wishes a single sub-continent or American Indian tribe, but if his inquiry is limited to that tribe alone, without reference to any other, anywhere else, he is not making a comparative study.

This is far from saying, of course, that the kind of study just referred to is not of interest to the student or researcher working comparatively. On the contrary, the accurate gathering and careful analysis of data from a single geographical or cultural situation is essential for him who works comparatively, whether the data he uses have been collected by himself or someone

[32] Ibid., p. 494.

41

else. The lack of a sufficient number of carefully conducted studies of different aspects and problems of librarianship, in different places and situations, has been a major deterrent to the development of a solid literature of comparative librarianship. It would not be possible, for example, for an investigator today to make, on the basis of existing documentation, a sound comparative study of the "medium-sized" public library in Germany and its sister institution in France simply because accurate and comparative data, in depth, on the administration, support, personnel, book stock, and use, of the medium-sized public library in the two countries are not available. The person who wished to make such a study would, therefore, have to gather his own information for both countries.

As already noted, Collings defines "area studies" as those "which provide a descriptive survey and a critical analysis of library development in a given country or region, in the context of relevant determinant back-ground factors," and she gives a number of examples which satisfactorily conform to this definition. She then writes: "Area studies usually deal with the contemporary scene but some are historical in nature such as Hassenforder's *Développement Comparé des Bibliothèques Publiques en France, en Grande-Bretagne et aux États-Unis . . . 1850–1915* [sic]."[33] By no possible stretch of the imagination can Hassenforder's very good study, one of a small handful of the kind that we have, be considered "a descriptive survey and a critical analysis of library development in a given country or region."

"Area studies" is probably as good a phrase as any to classify those works "which provide a descriptive survey and a critical analysis of library development in a given country" and the phrase should include, as for instance the *International Library Review* includes, studies involving aspects of librarianship in a single country or "area" as well as those covering all of librarianship in a given country or society. We need far more of them

[33] Ibid., pp. 494–95. The dates of the study are 1850–1914.

42

than we have. They will facilitate the work not only of the comparative investigator, but also of the student of the sociology and history of libraries. But, to repeat, such works are not themselves "comparative studies," and we should not confuse the issues and muddy our terminology by so designating them.

It may be suggested here that the often-used phrase "foreign librarianship" (*Auslandsbibliothekswesen, bibliothéconomie de l'étranger,* or, generically, "foreign studies," *Auslandskunde*) is coinage of questionable value. Years ago Friedrich Schneider pointed out the philosophical and semantic dilemma involved in the use of such phrases as *Auslandspädagogik,* "foreign education," and *pédagogie de l'étranger.* He observed that these phrases mean the education of foreign lands; therefore, for the citizen of any given country, education of all peoples excepting his own. Consequently, the concept of what is included in "foreign education" necessarily shifts according to the nationality of the person who uses or reads the phrase. Thus, he says, for the American, German pedagogy is "foreign" pedagogy, but can naturally not be so considered by the German, whereas American pedagogy is, equally, for the German, but not for the American, "foreign" pedagogy.[34] The same philosophical dilemma and objection apply to the use of such phrases as "foreign librarianship," "librarianship abroad," "foreign studies," and the like.

At the conclusion of her article, Collings rephrases her definition of case studies as those "which examine intensively a particular library problem or development in one country." (The distinction between this and "area studies, which provide a de-

[34] Friedrich Schneider, *Triebkräfte der Pädagogik der Völker* (Salzburg: Müller, 1947), p. 33. Schneider makes the same point, somewhat expanded, in his later work, *Vergleichende Erziehungswissenschaft* (Heidelberg: Quelle and Meyer, 1961), pp. 73–74, but continues to use the word *Auslandspädagogik* thereafter, probably because there is no very satisfactory substitute for it. For the same reason, "foreign librarianship" and the like have occasionally been used in this study, but always within quotation marks to remind the reader of the special connotation they carry.

scriptive survey and critical analysis of library development in a given country . . ." is very unclear.) Collings then cites, among other works, Lowell Martin's *Library Response to Urban Change: A Study of the Chicago Public Library* (Chicago: American Library Assn., 1969).[35] If we were, in fact, to admit Martin's study to the literature of comparative librarianship studies, there is hardly any work on any aspect of librarianship anywhere that could justifiably be excluded, and the corresponding definition of comparative librarianship would have lost totally all precision, meaning, and value.

1972

In a review article, Anthony Thompson appears to give tacit approval to Simsova's definitions of area studies and problem case studies, and then suggests: "either of these may be international if extended to more than one area; and I prefer the more ordinary words 'international' and 'inter-cultural' to her 'cross-national' and 'cross-cultural'."[36] Whether "inter-cultural" is a "more ordinary" word than "cross-cultural" seems open to question. What is not open to question is that "cross-cultural" has long been accepted and used to describe certain kinds of studies in the social sciences; it seems both unnecessary and unwise to propose, for librarianship, a much less commonly used word to describe studies involving two or more societies or cultures.

The same objection may be entered with regard to the use of "international" instead of "cross-national," but there is an additional reason here for not doing so. As considered later in this chapter, "international librarianship" can and should carry a special meaning, and our terminology will be more precise if we do not use the first word in the phrase in other contexts,

[35] Collings, "Comparative Librarianship," p. 495.

[36] Anthony Thompson, "Towards International Comparative Librarianship," *Journal of Librarianship* 4:68 (Jan. 1972).

even though the meaning of "international area study," which Thompson uses to describe one of the books he reviews, is no doubt clear enough.[37] At the beginning of his review, however, Thompson calls this same publication "an international comparative study," thus providing another example of the imprecision of our terminology.[38] The work referred to is not at all a "comparative study" and this kind of study is not the same as an area study.

There are three remarkable aspects about these definitions. The first is that they are all of Anglo-American origin. However, unless *Library Literature* and *Library and Information Science Abstracts* have been grossly derelict in noting and indexing our literature, librarians elsewhere have not interested themselves in the subject of comparative librarianship to the extent of writing about it.

The second noteworthy aspect about most of the definitions, foreshadowed in previous comment on some of them, may be summarized in the following way. Whether the definitions are (1) stipulative, that is, not directly reflective of prior usage, but either inventive, proposing a new terminology, or non-inventive, proposing a new meaning for existing terminology; or (2) descriptive, that is, explanatory, purporting accurately to reflect (but often violating) prior usage, they either (1) make the offered definitions dependent upon *specific* programs and purposes, or methodolgy, or (2) they are illogical, or (3) they are internally self-contradictory.[39] In other words, the definitions frequently posit or raise moral or practical questions which, however worthwhile and legitimate they may be, constitute a separate issue and should not determine our definitions; they are unreasonable; or they lack inner consistency.

[37] Ibid.

[38] Ibid., p. 57.

[39] *Cf.* Israel Scheffler, *The Language of Education* (Springfield, Ill.: Charles C. Thomas, c1960), pp. 12–35, whose discussion of this topic is gratefully acknowledged.

While there can be no criticism of inventive stipulative definitions, if intelligently arrived at, these may *not* at the same time be programmatic. Nor may a descriptive and explanatory definition wholly violate accepted prior usage. Clearly, definitions must also conform to simple logic and may not be self-contradictory. Disregard of these considerations has produced misleading and faulty statements and has resulted in the confused and imprecise situation we now have. What is needed is definition of our terms, preferably descriptive definitions in harmony with prior usage, but in any case definitions which are logical, consistent, divorced from programmatic and methodological elements, and which accurately characterize our concepts and terminology.

A third remarkable point about a majority of the definitions—a point not unrelated to the preceding one—is that they appear to have been developed *in vacuo*, without reference to the experience and findings of other disciplines. This observation applies particularly to the fact that many published definitions omit the *essentiality* either of a cross-national, cross-cultural, or cross-societal element, and of the juxtaposition and analysis of analogous phenomena, or they ignore the equally fundamental essence of comparative studies, namely the search for explanation and principle. Even a cursory examination of the literature of the most nearly similar social disciplines reveals virtually unanimous agreement on these three points, and those who, in speaking of comparative librarianship, choose to ignore, omit, or violate any of them are under a very heavy burden of justifying their position.

A source of the difficulty lies in the fact that a distinction has not been made between the field and the material of comparative librarianship, that is, in short, the total *subject* of comparative librarianship on the one hand, and comparative librarianship studies or research on the other. The two are not the same. Before considering this difficult and important point, support may be offered for the contention that the cross-societal

46

element, the juxtaposition of data, their actual comparison, and the search for explanations are indispensable elements of comparative studies in the social sciences.

Durkheim, for example, as early as the end of the last century, demonstrated that sociological explanation "consists entirely in the establishment of causal connections."[40]

The distinguished American comparative educator Isaac Kandel more than once stated the same basic contention, and on one occasion did so in these words: "Like the study of the history of education, comparative education seeks to discover underlying causes to explain why the educational systems of different countries differ from each other, what are their motivating aims and purposes, what their sources are, and what general principles may emerge."[41] (Emphasis added.)

Noah and Eckstein call the "cross-national dimension" one of the hallmarks "of work properly claiming to be comparative education" and note that "explanation is the ultimate aim of all scientific (and hence of all comparative) work in education."[42]

Jerome Hall, after reviewing the work of sociologists and legal scholars, makes clear the same points.[43]

H. C. Gutteridge writes:

> We may at once dismiss any such claim [regarding investigation into foreign law], so far as it relates to a mere compilation of facts concerning a single legal system, because in such a case there cannot be any comparison. Nor is such a claim enhanced merely because the compilation takes the form of a parallel or tabular statement of facts relating to

[40] Émile Durkheim, *Les Règles de la Méthode Sociologique* (Paris: Germer Baillière, 1895), p. 153 (my translation).

[41] Isaac L. Kandel, "The Study of Comparative Education," *Educational Forum* 20:5 (Nov. 1955).

[42] Harold J. Noah and Max Eckstein, *Toward a Science of Comparative Education* (New York: Macmillan, 1969), pp. 184, 187.

[43] Jerome Hall, *Comparative Law and Social Theory* (Baton Rouge: Louisiana State Univ. Pr., 1963), pp. 33–34.

several systems, which leaves it to a reader to discover for himself what differences may exist.[44]

Later he notes:

> The comparison must be based on a careful and accurate analysis of the foreign laws under investigation, but its most important aspect is the construction of a synthesis, founded on the results of the analytical process, which is intended to elucidate some problem either of an abstract or utilitarian character. The purpose of the comparison may be purely scientific. . . . This is also true of comparisons instituted . . . in aid of attempts to ascertain the concepts and principles which are to be found in all civilized systems of law.[45]

> . . . comparative education [writes William W. Brickman] is the . . . analysis of educational systems, issues, and problems in two or more countries within the context of historical, socioeconomic, political, cultural, religious, and other influential factors. . . . the task of the comparative educator, in the first instance, is full understanding and clear interpretation of the system or problem.[46]

"There can be no comparative education," writes C. Arnold Anderson, "without looking at different systems. . . . But this is only a beginning."

> The purpose of comparative education is to go further, to deal with complex systems of correlations among educational characteristics and between these and traits of social structure. . . . By convention, resting on solid meth-

[44] H. C. Gutteridge, *Comparative Law: An Introduction to the Comparative Method of Legal Study and Research* (Cambridge: Univ. Pr., 1946), p. 8.

[45] Ibid., p. 9.

[46] William W. Brickman, "Comparative Education," in *Encyclopedia of Educational Research* (1969), p. 184.

48

odological grounds, comparative study involves correlation across the boundaries of societies. . . .[47]

The ultimate aim of comparative education, like that of any other analysis of the social world, is knowledge of causation—if so quaint a word may be tolerated.[48]

Stewart E. Fraser and William W. Brickman, at the beginning of a major history of the subject, define comparative education as:

the analysis of educational systems and problems in two or more national environments in terms of socio-political, economic, cultural, ideological, and other contexts. Judgments are arrived at . . . to understand the factors, underlying similarities and differences in education in the various nations.[49]

Noting that comparison is an indispensable methodological means of all research, Leonhard Froese insists that the task and scope of comparative education lie under the perspective of a spatial requirement.[50] In a later, more specific definition, he says that "Vergleichende Erziehungswissenschaft ist jener Teil der Erziehungswissenschaft, der Phänomen, Problem, und Begriff der Erziehung bzw. Bildung in anderen geo-politischen und sozio-kulturellen Räumen zum Gegenstand einer synkritischen Analyse macht."[51] This may be freely translated as: "Compara-

---

[47] C. Arnold Anderson, "Methodology of Comparative Education," *International Review of Education* 7:6 (1961).

[48] Ibid., p. 4.

[49] Stewart E. Fraser and William W. Brickman, eds., *A History of International and Comparative Education* (Glenview, Ill.: Scott, Foresman, c1968), p. 1.

[50] Leonhard Froese, "Vergleichende Pädagogik," *Pädagogisches Lexikon* (Stuttgart: Kreuz-Verlag, 1961), cols. 695–97.

[51] Leonhard Froese, "Paradigmata des Selbstverständnisses der Vergleichenden Erziehungswissenschaft" (*Klausurtagung Marburg* 6./7. 1. 1967, No. 7).

tive education, or comparative educational science, is that part of the science of education which studies phenomena, problems, and concepts of education in other geo-political and socio-cultural areas with the objective of syncretic analysis."

Throughout his extensive, book-length review of comparative studies in sociology, Robert M. Marsh more than once emphasizes that "cross-societal (cross-cultural, cross-national) comparison is the essential ingredient" and says that "Comparative sociology has the task of progressively specifying which theories, propositions, etc. hold for all societies, which for only certain classes or types of societies, and which for only individual societies."[52]

Franz Hilker notes:

> Often a study or report upon a single foreign educational situation is spoken of as a contribution to comparative education. . . . Such a study can be a good and necessary preparation for a comparative investigation. This last, however, exists only when two or more objects of the same or similar kind are placed in juxtaposition.[53]

Finally, a recent definition:

> Comparative educations is that branch of the theory of education concerned with the analysis and interpretation of educational practices and policies in different countries and cultures. . . . The aim . . . is to explain why things

[52] Robert M. Marsh, "Comparative Sociology, 1950–1963. A Trend Report and Bibliography," *Current Sociology* 14, no. 2:5, 6 (1966). Numerous other writers, from various disciplines, could be cited on the importance and necessity of establishing causal connections and attempting to arrive at principles. Mention may be made of A. R. Radcliffe-Brown, *A Natural Science of Society* (Glencoe, Ill.: Free Pr., c1957); and Max Weber, *The Methodology of the Social Sciences*, trans. by Edward A. Shils and Henry A. Finch (Glencoe, Ill.: Free Pr., 1949), esp. pp. 79–80.

[53] Franz Hilker, *Vergleichende Pädagogik* (Munich: Hueber, 1962), p. 103 (my translation).

are as they are. The hope is to provide a body of principles. . . .[54]

The distinction between what is "comparative" and what is not, therefore, is quite clear-cut; regardless of other factors, such as quality, authorship, motivation, or sponsorship; (1) actual comparison, (2) a cross-national, cross-societal, or cross-cultural element, and (3) explanation of observed differences must be present. A study of the school libraries of Denmark today, no matter by whom or how formed, is not a comparative study so long as the school libraries of no other countries are included.

But "country" itself is not a necessarily determining criterion. A study of school library financial support and use in French-speaking and English-speaking Quebec is a legitimate comparative study, because these two parts of the province have been shaped by diverse traditions, cultures, and social forces, and the social institutions produced by them will necessarily be somewhat different. Comparative also, and for the same reason, would be a study of public libraries of French- and German-speaking Switzerland.

In the same way, some areas of Africa provide instances of a people influenced by two different cultures. An example is the western and eastern Ewe of former German Togoland. In 1919 the western part was given to Great Britain, the eastern to France, so that for nearly half a century these two countries set the educational and cultural influences of their respective territories. Even though the areas are now independent, the influences still persist.

As a not too far removed analogy, the anthropologist could justifiably claim that his study, in an earlier day, of two American Indian tribes was a comparative one, because their isolation from each other, and the lack of communication between them produced quite different traditions, customs, and language.

[54] J. A. Lauwerys, "Comparative Education," in Edward Blishen, ed., *Encyclopedia of Education* (New York: Philosophical Library, 1970), p. 152.

When similarities in one or another of these respects were observed, the cause had to be sought elsewhere than in cross-societal impact.

In light of all the foregoing, and in an attempt to arrive at a working, logical, and defensible terminology, it is not merely useful, but essential to make a distinction, alluded to earlier, between the field or subject of comparative librarianship as a total complex, on the one hand, and as a matter of scholarly inquiry and research, on the other. The *field* properly includes almost everything embraced in Collings's multifaceted definition. It includes, that is, case and area studies of single societies; what is commonly called "foreign librarianship"; the collection of data about libraries, or aspects of librarianship in "other" countries; and the study of library development, practices, problems, and the like in different countries.

The obviously much more narrow and restricted area of scholarly investigation and research may be defined as the analysis of libraries, library systems, some aspect of librarianship, or library problems in two or more national, cultural, or societal environments, in terms of socio-political, economic, cultural, ideological, and historical contexts. This analysis is for the purpose of understanding the underlying similarities and differences, and for determining explanations of the differences, with the ultimate aim of trying to arrive at valid generalizations and principles. In both the field as a total complex and in scholarly investigation, data and documents will inevitably be used, and considerations taken account of, that are not themselves either cross-societal or comparative.

Friedrich Schneider, among others, makes a somewhat similar distinction for education between "foreign education" (*Auslandspädagogik*) and "comparative education" (*Vergleichende Erziehungswissenschaft*), and limits use of the latter term to scholarly study involving the systematic application of comparative method.[55]

[55] Schneider, *Vergleichende Erziehungswissenschaft*, p. 74.

Another distinguished comparative educator, Pedro Rossello, notes that works on comparative education usually present two different facets: on the one hand, *descriptive* comparative education (collection of documents, observation and comparison of facts in order to describe differences and similarities); on the other hand, *explanatory* comparative education (investigation of the causes of the comparative phenomena and, if possible, predictions as to their future development).[56]

It is clear that we cannot expect, at the level of beginning instruction *about* comparative librarianship, that causes and explanations will be newly discovered or principles determined. But even here, one dare not lose sight of the ultimate, long-range goal. And even here, what is described as "comparative" must truly be so and must embrace a cross-national, cross-cultural, or cross-societal element.

One other concept, "international librarianship," calls for discussion and definition. The term is widely used—though seldom defined—in our literature. "International librarianship" and "comparative librarianship" are sometimes used synonymously (e.g., under 1970a above), and in at least one instance, comparative librarianship has been held to be "a sub-discipline of the general subject of international librarianship" (citation under 1969 above). As the preceding discussion has shown, "comparative librarianship" is a quite specific concept, of which two closely related aspects may be distinguished. We should not becloud our terminology by confusing the concept with some other. There is a satisfactory role and place for "international librarianship."

The appellation "international" is known in other fields as well, viz., "international education" and "international law." It must be said that, until fairly recently at least, librarianship was not alone in often using the terms "comparative" and

---

[56] Pedro Rossello, *L'éducation Comparée au Service de la Planification,* Les Cahiers de Pédagogie Expérimentale et de Psychologie de L'enfant, n.s., no. 17 (Neuchâtel: Delachaux and Niestlé, c1959), p. 2.

"international" synonymously. Fraser and Brickman point out, for example, that "Kandel used the two terms interchangeably, as can be seen in his classic introductory work, *Comparative Education* (1933). Moreover, Carter V. Good's *Dictionary of Education* (1959) treats them synonymously. Nevertheless," they add, "one should be aware of the differences in meaning in order to make use in writing and discussion more clear and reliable."[57]

> International Education connotes the various kinds of relationships—intellectual, cultural, and educational—among individuals and groups from two or more nations. It is a dynamic concept in that it involves a movement across frontiers, whether by a person, book, or idea. International education refers to the various methods of international cooperation, understanding, and exchange. Thus, the exchange of teachers and students, aid to underdeveloped countries, and teaching about foreign educational systems fall within the scope of this term.[58]

If we substitute in this quotation for the words "education" and "educational" the words "librarianship" and "library," we have a highly satisfactory definition of "international librarianship." The use of the term is perfectly exemplified by the names and activities of the International Relations Committee, the International Relations Office, and the International Relations Round Table of the American Library Association.

There is a final issue that needs to be explored. Although, as noted, almost all of those who have attempted to define the comparative insist upon a spatial, cross-cultural or cross-national element, a few would include a time element as well. Hilker, for example, speaks of the possibility, that is, the legitimacy, of examining professional education in Germany in 1850, 1900, and

[57] Fraser and Brickman, *History*, p. 1, f. 1.
[58] Ibid., p. 1.

54

1950.[59] Maurice Duverger also advances the possibility of studying phenomena of the same kind that are separated by time, and gives as an illustration "the French Parliament under Louis-Philippe, between 1875 and 1914, between the two wars, in the Fourth and Fifth Republics."[60]

Although these views are minority ones, and suggest a philosophical question, some defense of them can certainly be made. That is, the "societies" of the 1850s and the 1950s in the United States were undoubtedly more different than, say, the societies of Norway and Sweden are today. If, therefore, we are primarily concerned, in comparative studies, in studying phenomena of analogous kinds in different social contexts, perhaps we should admit that such a study might be limited to a single geographical area at different times, provided it can be shown that these times are socially significantly different. (The single-area, single-geography, single-nation studies in librarianship claiming to be comparative have almost without exception involved a single time period, the "present," or contemporary.)

There is, however, an important counter-argument. This kind of vertical, or chronological study of a single society, whether the conditions of one time period are directly compared with those of another or not, has commonly and for long been considered the province of the library historian, just as such vertical, or chronological study in education or government has traditionally been left to the historians in those fields. The comparativist's claim for including them in his territory does not seem overly strong, and the claim is further weakened when one considers a major advantage which the comparativist has often advanced for his approach. He usually speaks, nowadays at least, of examining personally the present-day workings of the

[59] Hilker, *Vergleichende Pädagogik*, p. 103.

[60] Maurice Duverger, *An Introduction to the Social Sciences, with Special Reference to Their Methods*, trans. by Malcolm Anderson (London: Allen and Unwin, 1964), p. 262.

bar, the school systems, the forms of government, or the libraries of two or more societies. He consults with those in posts of responsibility or in a position to know. He attends international meetings where problems and status are being discussed. He mails out questionnaires. None of this is possible except for the present. All of it makes possible for the comparativist a kind of research and research result which is not open to the historian, so long as he is studying something which happened earlier than the lifetimes of men now living.

The issue clearly is not a black and white one, and it is not one to which additional fact can be brought to bear for the answer. It is probably, as much as anything, a philosophical question. On balance, it would seem to the writer that the vertical, or chronological, study of a single society might better be left to the historian.[61]

The point just discussed, perhaps as much a question of scope as of definition, leads us to a consideration of the former topic.

Librarianship, like any other discipline, is obliged to give thought to the territory which it considers, and can defend, as its own. In fact, legitimate doubt will always exist concerning the scholarly and academic nature of a field which is unable to state with some clarity what its territory is. This is as true for comparative librarianship as it has been for librarianship as a whole.

Despite differences in detail and emphasis even within a given country, the curricula of library education agencies represent the consensus, at least of library educators, as to what librarianship is all about and of what its essentials consist. This consensus has not easily been achieved; on the contrary, it has

[61] Writers in other fields have come to the same conclusion. For example, William W. Brickman, following a discussion of the topic, makes the statement: "The comparative studies within a single country and the comparative historical studies do not fall within the scope of Comparative Education as understood by most workers in the field." ("The Theoretical Foundations of Comparative Education," *The Journal of Educational Sociology* 30:124 [Nov. 1956].)

been the result of much soul-searching, and as knowledge increased, as new technologies developed and social conditions changed, so too have come changes in what has been deemed to be the essential territory of library education, and hence of librarianship.

The territory of comparative studies, and not in librarianship alone, presents a still more difficult problem precisely because such studies are cross-cultural and inter-disciplinary.

Very little has been written, except in the most general terms, on the scope of comparative librarianship, and what has been written has been cited in this chapter. It does not seem enough to say, simply, that the territory of comparative librarianship is "the study and comparison of library theory and practice in all of the different countries of the world."[62]

Clearly the territory of comparative librarianship is where certain other disciplines, chiefly the social sciences, but sometimes, also, the humanities, librarianship itself, and a cross-societal dimension intersect. But two problems arise. The first is whether it is possible to distinguish an inquiry in comparative librarianship from, say, an inquiry in comparative government, if the problem being investigated concerns the governance of a certain kind of library in two or more societies.

It is the writer's judgment that the answer to the indirect question is a qualified yes. Obviously a political scientist could claim such a study as lying within his scope. But if the purpose of this inquiry is to discover something about the relationship between governance and library service, that is, if the end result is a library, rather than a political science matter, then the comparative librarian might claim to have a prior territorial interest over the political scientist. The same kind of argument and conclusion apply to studies having primarily sociological and

[62] Louis Shores, "Why Comparative Librarianship?" *Wilson Library Bulletin* 41:204 (Oct. 1966). See also, Miles M. Jackson, Jr., "Libraries Abroad," *The Journal of Library History* 1:133 (Apr. 1966), for a very similar statement.

economic bases. Examples would be: inquiries into ethnic factors influencing public library use; and the effect of varying tax bases upon public library support.

In one sense, at least, this discussion might be considered somewhat academic. In Western society, fortunately, there is nothing whatever to prevent anyone from addressing himself to any inquiry that interests him, and he may study any matter he pleases even though his competence, and his resources of time, money, and materials are quite insufficient to prosecute the undertaking satisfactorily. In a free society this is inevitable and, in the long run, beneficial. It is wholly against the assumptions of Western learning today to erect barriers against the "quest for truth" by anyone for any reason.

On the other hand, the question is by no means entirely an academic one. We certainly need, as suggested above, to have some notion of the bounds of our area for guidance in our own work, and for the information of others. Equally important, a clear understanding of these bounds leads us to a recognition of our responsibilities as a serious discipline, vis-à-vis the responsibilities of others. Thus, assuming that it is important to society and the advancement of knowledge for us to know something about the relationship between the governance and the service of public libraries in different societies, we cannot logically assume that the inquiry will be made by political scientists, and, if we make the assumption, we will, much more often than not, be disappointed. This is part of the territory for which we, the library profession, should assume primary responsibility.

This in no sense implies an intention of establishing a closed frontier between us and the other social sciences. On the contrary, we need far greater cross-fertilization and co-operation between those doing comparative, as well as other kinds of work, in librarianship, and those working in other disciplines. The question is solely one of special interest, special concern, specialization, and principal responsibility.

Although it is mainly the social sciences that come into play in studies of all kinds concerned with the library as a social institution, there are studies of other sorts which must inevitably draw upon different disciplines. A comparative examination of cataloging codes, subject headings, or classification schemes, particularly if they were in different languages, would probably need to draw upon logic and linguistics, especially semantics. One can certainly conceive of studies in librarianship that would involve architecture, engineering, or law. A comparative inquiry into the influence of climate upon the design of library buildings not only must take some account of the first of these but, also, of climatology, as anyone can testify who has studied good library buildings in parts of the world that have excessively hot sunshine and high temperatures. Glass panel walls on the southern exposure of a library building in Southeast Asia come close to being an impossibility.

While it may be an act of temerity to intimate that there is any discipline which might not be pertinent to some study or other in librarianship, it seems safe to suggest that most of the physical and biological sciences will seldom, if ever, come into question. It is, for example, difficult to imagine comparative studies which would be required to draw upon biochemistry, botany, genetics, immunology, nutrition, paleontology, plant pathology, chemistry, endocrinology, molecular biology, or plant physiology.

A second issue regarding scope may be raised by asking whether all aspects of libraries and librarianship, so long as cross-societal and cross-disciplinary elements are involved, are properly encompassed in the territory of comparative librarianship. Logic, as well as the views, experience, and activities of comparative educators, among others, suggests an affirmative answer. Even if librarianship were the first rather than one of the last disciplines seriously to embrace comparative studies, and we consequently lacked other experience and guides, logic would dictate the affirmative response. It would do so simply because there appears to be no sound basis upon which we might say that this, that, or some other aspect of libraries and librarianship should be *excluded*. Library service to different kinds of people, library education, buildings, financial support, book collections, administrative organization, reader interests, staff—what possible criteria might we set up which would warrant excluding any one of these or the almost infinite number of other areas, topics, subjects, questions, and so on, of concern to the profession and society? No such criteria seem logically or practically defensible.

This, however, is obviously not at all the same as saying that everything which might be studied comparatively (or in any other way for that matter) is worth study. One speaks with considerable caution here, since the history of scholarship is replete with examples of inquiries, generally viewed with scorn at the time, which later proved to be of substantial value. Nonetheless, *reductio ad absurdum*, one might without too much temerity suggest that some questions are almost certainly not worth studying. It does not seem likely, for instance, that knowledge derived from testing the following hypothesis would be worth gaining: "The use of green-colored call-slips in the school libraries of North Country has resulted in greater use of school library books, compared with use in the school libraries of South Country, where the call-slips are gray." To one who wished to defend an investigation of this nature, we could at least point out with some confidence that the study of a great many other problems would be more likely to produce knowledge commensurate with the time and effort expended.

It is necessary to consider, too, the question of scope from a different point of view, namely that of the field as a total subject, as discussed earlier in this chapter. Scope in this sense refers to the totality of the elements encompassed in the field. Consequently, the scope of the whole subject of comparative librarianship includes all kinds of documentation about libraries and librarianship necessary for comparative study; area and case studies; teaching about libraries and librarianship in "other" countries; and those aspects of international librarianship, as earlier defined, which are relevant to or supportive of comparative librarianship.

A final aspect of scope, or a limitation, and one concerned with purpose, should be noted. It will be recalled from the quotations cited at the beginning of this chapter that some of those who have written about comparative librarianship have stated that among its aims or purposes should be moral improvement and determination of values. This is completely contrary to the accepted view of science in general and of scholarly inquiry in the social sciences in particular. The comparative method, discussed in detail in chapter 5, is an empirically grounded means of discovery concerned with the "what is," given existing library realities. It seeks to study these through, and in relationship to, the sociological, political, economic, historical, and cultural conditions in which they are found, and by which they have been produced. This means for discovering new knowledge is not and cannot be concerned with "what should be" in a value sense. It is not, that is, concerned with the library ideals toward which we should strive. Questions in this area, which might be summed up in the phrase "library philosophy," must, indeed, be left to the philosophers.

"Comparative Education," notes Lauwerys, "is not normative: it does not prescribe rules for the good conduct of schools and teaching. It does not lay down what should be done: it tries instead to understand what is done and why, taking into account ideology as well as socio-economic background and racial, national and religious prejudices."[63]

A careful distinction, however, should be drawn here so as not to exclude a large and important, somewhat related area of inquiry, which quite properly lies within the scope of comparative studies. A specific example, and one as closely akin as pos-

[63] J. A. Lauwerys, "Comparative Education," p. 152. Numerous social scientists make the same point. See, e.g., Max Weber, *Methodology of the Social Sciences*, pp. 52–59.

sible to the excluded realm just discussed, may be suggested for illustration.

Assume the existence, in two societies, of two different standards, A and B, for the provision of books for "small" public libraries. Assume, further, that the libraries of the two countries have consistently followed these standards. Assume, finally, that a satisfactory study, with all necessary controls, could be set up to test the hypothesis that "under certain given conditions, standard A would produce more books wanted by more patrons than would standard B because. . . ." If, then, the results of the study supported the truth of the proposition, we should be quite justified in saying that, given such and such conditions, it would be better for libraries to follow standard A *if* an aim of their book provision policy is to produce the largest number of books desired by the most people. This is not a value judgment, and the comparativist, or other competent practitioner, may properly be called upon to implement the standard. A related value judgment, which is not within the province of comparative studies, would be that this *should* be the aim, or an aim, of the book selection policy, or that some other aim would be a "better" one.

3

The Dimensions of Purpose and Value

Almost all previous writers about the nature of comparative librarianship have expressed opinions concerning the purposes for which studies are or should be undertaken, and the values and benefits to be derived from them. While some of these statements naturally have elements in common, they differ radically from each other in the number and kind of purposes and benefits described and, most particularly and disturbingly, in the emphases and priorities the authors set forth. The principal views we have available are considered in the following paragraphs, arranged chronologically.

As statements of purpose and value are sometimes inextricably bound up with those of definition, it has not always been possible to eliminate all elements of the latter from the quotations which follow. There is, therefore, some unavoidable repetition of material presented in the preceding chapter. Such repetition, however, has the advantage of amplifying and placing in context the cited statements. For the most part, comment on them appears following the last one.

1954a

The purpose of comparative librarianship, Chase Dane writes, is "to discover what factors are common to [certain] countries and which are unique to one. It is an evaluation of the philosophies and policies of librarianship on an international scale to determine long-range trends, to appraise shortcomings, and to uncover contradictions and inconsistencies between practice and theory."[1]

1954b

In a second article, Dane suggests that the purpose of comparative librarianship is to discover, through a study of library development in many countries, "what developments have been successful and can be copied elsewhere," and, through "an examination of the philosophies and policies of librarianship on an international scale to determine long-range trends, to appraise shortcomings, and to uncover contradictions and inconsistencies between practice and theory. Above all it is the study of the cause and effect of library development throughout the world. . . . comparative librarianship seeks to broaden our tolerance and deepen our understanding."[2] Following this general statement, Dane describes in greater detail the following benefits:

1. Discovery of the best "methods and techniques for organizing library materials and for making these materials available to readers," leading to the introduction of "the best [methods] into countries which do not use them"
2. Re-evaluation of the philosophy of librarianship and sharpening of librarians' "thinking about some of the fundamental problems of their profession"

[1] Chase Dane, "The Benefits of Comparative Librarianship," *The Australian Library Journal*, 3:89 (July 1954).

[2] Chase Dane, "Comparative Librarianship," *The Librarian and Book World*, 43:141 (Aug. 1954).

3. The eventual creation of "a unified philosophy of library service. . . . capable of adapting itself to almost any situation and . . . devoid of the inconsistencies and disagreements which now characterize much of our thinking about librarianship"
4. "The widespread adoption of sound policies"
5. "Improved universal bibliographic control"
6. The free flow and free exchange of ideas between librarians
7. The bringing of library service in "small or backward countries . . . up to the same standards as that in large countries."[3]

1958

The stated aims of a graduate seminar in comparative librarianship, developed by Dorothy Collings, are:

1. To study available data concerning the library systems, problems and solutions of selected countries, in the light of their particular circumstances;
2. To gain perspective on, and added insight into, the library problems which obtain in one's own situation;
3. To assist in the development of data and techniques for the comparative study of librarianship;
4. To assist in the advancement of international cooperation in the field of library development.[4]

1964

In a paper published this year, Carl M. White says, "the purpose of this chapter is to use [the comparative] method to identify some of the common characteristics, or tendencies, which emerge from empirical study of the three nations [Britain, Ger-

---

[3] Ibid., pp. 142–43.

[4] Dorothy Collings, "Meeting the Needs of Foreign Students," *Library Journal* 83:3064 (Nov. 1, 1958).

many, and the United States] named above."⁵ This, as far as it goes, is a defensible purpose, but it hardly needs to be pointed out that identification of "common characteristics or tendencies," is not enough; it is not the be-all and end-all of comparative studies.

Other purposes are not noted—but there was no reason for White to list others, as he undoubtedly would have had he been writing with a different objective.

1965a

The comparative method, writes D. J. Foskett, is used to study the past "in order to discover patterns of progress in given social situations, for the purpose of measuring such patterns against other patterns, to see their similarities and differences. . . . In a practical activity such as librarianship a better understanding of the activity under different circumstances cannot help but influence future planning."⁶

1965b

"What we are trying to do, in comparative studies," Foskett suggests in another article, "is to unravel the strands that go to make up a certain pattern, to assess these strands against those that make up other, different, patterns, and to try to form estimates of the relative values of each."⁷

Thus the objects of comparative studies cover the whole field of an activity. In librarianship, our first preoccupation

⁵ Carl M. White, "Comparative Study of Library Systems," in Carl M. White, ed., *Bases of Modern Librarianship* (Oxford: Pergamon Pr., 1964), p. 13.

⁶ D. J. Foskett, "Comparative Librarianship," *The Library World*, 66: 296 (June 1965).

⁷ D. J. Foskett, "Comparative Librarianship," in Robert L. Collison, ed., *Progress in Library Science, 1965* (London: Butterworths, 1965), p. 126.

may well be to aim at a fuller understanding of the social role of libraries, but since, like education, it is a practical activity, such fuller understanding is bound to influence future planning. . . .[8]

These quotations, out of context, do not do full justice to Foskett's thoughtful article, which points out the importance of comparative studies as a means of systematizing observations and arriving at decisions based upon testable hypotheses rather than opinions. There is much else of great merit, and, in fact, the article is a fuller and better statement of what comparative librarianship is all about than most which have appeared since. Nonetheless, the major aim of comparative studies is not "to form estimates of the relative values" of different patterns. Value judgments, in the strict meaning of the phrase, at any rate, have no place in comparative studies.

1966a

Lester Asheim, in his interesting and provocative *Librarianship in the Developing Countries* (Urbana: Univ. of Illinois Pr., 1966), does not specifically speak to the purposes of comparative librarianship, but he presents a number of instructive comparisons and contrasts, and suggests throughout the lectures that make up the volume, that international and comparative inquiry is primarily concerned with the objective examination of problems and differences, and with the promotion of the useful exchange of information and ideas. He also discusses the role of the "foreign" expert abroad.

1966b

According to Miles M. Jackson, comparative librarianship is "that field of study that deals with the comparison of the theory and practice of librarianship in different countries, for the pur-

[8] Ibid., p. 127.

pose of deepening and broadening understanding of problems beyond national boundaries."[9] This is not only too limited a statement of purpose, but it also omits the principal purposes, discussed hereafter.

1966c

A very similar purpose, stated by Louis Shores in the same year, is that "of broadening and deepening our understanding of professional problems and solutions."[10] The comment following the preceding quotation applies here, too.

1966d

A New York State University conference produced the following view: "Research in international comparative librarianship could play a major part in developing for the profession a more articulate and realistic conception of the social role and vital functions of librarianship."[11]

1968a

Jean Hassenforder traces some of the history of comparative studies in librarianship, with particular reference to public librarianship and, after suggesting that there is now a relative abundance of information and description which can be drawn upon, expresses the opinion that comparison provides a "basis for better understanding," that "it is also productive of more effective action at the practical level," and that "what is still needed is a

[9] Miles M. Jackson, Jr., "Libraries Abroad," The Journal of Library History, 1:133 (Apr. 1966).

[10] Louis Shores, "Why Comparative Librarianship?" Wilson Library Bulletin, 41:204 (Oct. 1966).

[11] "The Research Rationale for International Comparative Librarianship" (Discussion paper presented at a faculty conference of the New York State University held at Oyster Bay, N.Y., 1966), pp. 1–2.

fuller analysis of the connections between the political, economic, social and cultural factors operative in the evolution of societies and the development of public libraries. As a result of the progress achieved in the human sciences studies of this kind are now beginning to appear and with the richer material to be found in them, comparisons of real significance can be established." In a concluding section, the author notes that "Comparative studies help us to a better understanding of the phases and modalities of library development."[12]

1968b

In the interests of international understanding [says Nasser Sharify] comparative courses are needed showing the relationship between libraries or information centers and the societies that create them, and which they in turn must serve. But, in order to be able to compare, one has to develop a comparative methodology and establish reliable data. The study of the development of libraries in other countries will shed light on the national library development of one's own country. The close relationship between library development and social, cultural, economic and educational development is fully realized only when one studies these developments within the framework of various cultures.[13]

1970a

John Roe has written of international and comparative librarianship activities in Great Britain, including the introduction, in 1966, of separate courses on comparative librarianship

[12] Jean Hassenforder, "Comparative Studies and the Development of Public Libraries," UNESCO Bulletin for Libraries 22:13, 15 and 18 (Jan.-Feb. 1968).

[13] Nasser Sharify, "The Need for Change in Present Library Science Curricula," in Larry E. Bone, ed., Library Education: An International Survey (Champaign: Univ. of Illinois Graduate School of Library Science, 1968), p. 182.

in library schools, and has noted that "all these postgraduate courses place special emphasis on project work, concerning area or problem studies considered cross-nationally or cross-culturally. Not only does the subject provide excellent educational functions but the practical implications add an extra appeal, and overseas students in particular get the chance to look closely at their country's needs and provision. Because of the success with this new focus in library studies, the Library Association has included a new paper, B37 (International and Comparative Librarianship) in its two-year course syllabus. . . ."[14]

1970b

The aims of a proposed introductory, but graduate-level course on "International-Comparative Librarianship," suggested by Martin H. Sable and Lourdes Deya are stated as follows:

1) To introduce students to specific socio-economic-political and cultural data of given foreign nations as background material for international-comparative librarianship.

2) To make the student aware of the potentials of the international and comparative aspects of librarianship, and as a result to broaden his outlook, specifically to understand and adjust to the values systems of other cultures.

3) As a result of this international perspective, the student may be motivated to enhance his qualifications for international librarianship through advanced work in language and area studies.

4) A question has arisen as to whether librarianship is a profession. To the extent that librarianship becomes international and develops a body of theory international in flavor, in the same measure and simultaneous with development of theory in other fields of librarianship will library science truly become a profession.

[14] John Roe, "International and Comparative Librarianship Activities," *Library Association Record* 72:266 (July 1970).

5) To gain a sharper insight into U.S. librarianship as a result of the comparative study.[15]

None of these aims is unworthy, but the principal purposes and values of comparative study are omitted.

1970c

It is difficult to distill from Shores's paper published in this year a precise set of purposes, but the following quotations give the tenor and approach of the article on this point:

> Although the proximate thesis here is that librarianship as a profession can best improve itself by comparative study, the ultimate thesis is that our professional destiny is to lead this troubled world out of its current dilemmas by teaching people everywhere to compare their ideals and their societies.[16]

> But our profession and its discipline can never reach their high destiny until they begin to compare more significantly. Librarians the world over can never assume their decisive role until librarianship becomes comparative.[17]

> [Comparative librarianship has] the purpose of broadening and deepening our understanding of professional problems and solutions.[18]

> Comparative librarianship offers a qualitative measure of our contemporary brand of intellectual freedom.[19]

How? The intended meaning here is very obscure.

[15] Martin H. Sable and Lourdes Deya, "Outline of an Introductory Course in International and Comparative Librarianship," *International Library Review* 2:187, 188–89 (Apr. 1970).

[16] Louis Shores, "Comparative Librarianship: A Theoretical Approach," in Miles M. Jackson, Jr., ed., *Comparative and International Librarianship* (Westport, Conn.: Greenwood, 1970), p. 4.

[17] Ibid., p. 4.

[18] Ibid., p. 5.

[19] Ibid., p. 7.

> Qualitative analysis [of book circulation figures] can be said to approach the mission of Comparative Librarianship.[20]

This statement, if taken at face value, is, at the least, far too restrictive.

> If libraries could anticipate issues that stimulate violence, lure potential marchers off the streets and into reading rooms to document problems, and identify solutions so superior that their adoption would irresistibly overcome current social evils, then Comparative Librarianship would be approaching its own high role.[21]

This is not the "high role" of any kind of comparative study.

1970d

In the same year Shores published another paper, in which he repeated his view of the purpose of comparative librarianship as being that of "broadening and deepening our understanding of problems and solutions."[22] The article stresses the value of comparisons in gaining knowledge about other, "better" library procedures and ways of solving library problems, and cites several British views and practices which, in Shores's opinion, are superior to prevailing American ones.

1970e

Sylvia Simsova does not directly state her view of the purpose of comparative librarianship, but seems to suggest its practical usefulness "as a tool for cultural borrowing and as a tool for bringing order into material (and thinking) about librarianship."[23]

[20] Ibid., p. 12.

[21] Ibid., p. 13.

[22] Louis Shores, "Librarian, Know Yourself," *Canadian Library Journal* 27:451 (Nov.-Dec. 1970).

[23] S. Simsova and M. MacKee, A *Handbook of Comparative Librarianship* (London: Bingley, c1970), p. 15.

1971

Dorothy Collings suggests that comparative librarianship

> constitutes an important approach to the search for cause and effect in library development, and to the understanding of library problems. . . . it is concerned primarily with providing a clearer view of current library problems and the process of library development. . . . [Its basic preoccupation is] with the systematic search for accurate understanding and interpreting of library practices and results in different cultural contexts. . . .
>
> As stated above, the basic purpose of comparative librarianship as a subject of scholarly concern is to seek full understanding and correct interpretation of the library system or problem under review.

Other pragmatic goals are:

(1) to provide guidelines for a proposed new library program in one's own country or in a foreign country;

(2) to contribute to the critical analysis and solution of widely-found library problems, viewed in their respective contexts;

(3) to stimulate and assist judicious consideration and possible adaptation of promising practices and solutions to library problems from one area to another while guarding against indiscriminate emulation;

(4) to provide background information for use in foreign library work assignments, study visits, consultation, or aid programs;

(5) to facilitate exchanges of library materials or information, particularly among different countries;

(6) to strengthen the scholarly content and practical relevance of library education and training, both for national and foreign students, through the consideration of library development and problems in differing cultural contexts; and

(7) to contribute to the advancement of international understanding and more extensive and effective cooperation in library planning and development.[24]

[24] Dorothy G. Collings, "Comparative Librarianship," in *Encyclopedia of Library and Information Science*, 5:492–94.

Collings's summation of benefits and uses is by far the most precise and complete that we have. In her statements that comparative librarianship "constitutes an important approach to the search for cause and effect in library development," that its basic preoccupation is "with the systematic search for accurate understanding and interpreting of library practices and results in differing cultural contexts," and that "the basic purpose of comparative librarianship as a subject of scholarly concern is to seek full understanding and correct interpretation of the library system or problem under review," we have the elements of (1) the most important purpose and (2) the overriding criteria of all comparative studies in social fields: the search for generally applicable principles which will explain observed phenomena; and the idea of a cross-national, cross-cultural, or cross-geographical content and scope.

Brief, general comment is offered on these opinions, following which these and other specific purposes, benefits, and values of comparative studies in librarianship are discussed in some detail.

Like the definitions cited in chapter 2, these opinons regarding purpose and benefit are noteworthy in that they all—with a single exception—come from Anglo-American writers, and that a majority of the views have been developed without reference to the experience and findings of other disciplines. In particular, with only two or three exceptions, the statements omit entirely the primary (non-programmatic) purpose or aim of all serious comparative work, namely, the search for explanation, or knowledge of causation, and for principles. This point was considered at some length in the preceding chapter and need not be further discussed here. However, it cannot be too strongly stressed that the largest purpose, the ultimate aim, is knowledge about the relationships of the phenomena we observe, and not a listing or description of them, no matter what other useful purposes such listing and description may serve.

Turning now to specific and programmatic benefits of comparative studies, it seems probable that careful and intensive

74

study on a broad geographical scale of library practices and procedures will result in the general adoption of the "better" ones, given a certain set of circumstances and conditions. This potential and indirect benefit, and those immediately following, may result, *even though they are not the purposes of the studies*. Examples abound of widely differing, indeed diametrically opposed, *practices* in library *situations* which are not basically dissimilar: free versus closed access to book collections in university libraries; conflicting rules for catalog main entries of governmental and other non-personal authors and for serial publications; close versus broad book classification; the various kinds and levels of library education as exemplified in Germany, the United Kingdom, and the United States. Every experienced librarian could add to this list. It is not suggested that scholarly investigation of the causes, results, and implications of these differing practices would necessarily result in the use of a single, generally applicable "best" answer. It is claimed, however, that no such study has been made of these or scores of other important practices, that study might reveal some guiding or controlling principles, and that it might lead to the adoption in some places of demonstrably better procedures, given a particular set of circumstances and conditions.

Comparative studies will also reveal completely new, or modified techniques, which may be beneficially introduced elsewhere. An example is the use of facsimile reproduction, over telephone lines, as a substitute for inter-library loan. The variations on the modular plan of construction, in the recently completed building of the University of Frankfurt Library, appear to be little known or understood outside of Germany, and the effects of these variations have not been carefully assessed even there. The results, in terms of who reads what and how much, of the two contrasting philosophies of public library book selection, namely, give the reader/taxpayer everything he wants, versus give him what the library thinks he should have, have similarly never been carefully evaluated.

There can be little doubt that comparative studies will broaden the professional viewpoint of those who make them, and that this broadening will almost surely result, at least to some extent, in greater general awareness, and hence in an enhanced professional contribution. Everyone who has engaged in international and comparative studies, even at an unsophisticated level of pure narration and description, and who has testified on the point, concedes this broadening benefit. The thoughtful student or observer cannot help but be stimulated by finding a new problem, a new situation, a new practice, a different solution to an old problem, or a modification or variation of an already known practice.

This in turn, more often than not, gains for the student or observer an added or different perspective on, and a better understanding of, the library situation with which he is most familiar. It is frequently a salutary experience for a librarian, particularly one from the Anglo-American world, which has long considered itself pre-eminent in many aspects of library practice and organization, to realize that other ways of doing things, other means for achieving stated goals, have strong arguments in their favor and may, under certain conditions, be superior to hitherto accepted practices and methods.

Some of the purposes/benefits suggested in the preceding paragraphs clearly have strong implications for library planning, and we have abundant written testimony that developments and innovations in library architecture, the mechanical construction or reproduction of catalogs, and administrative procedures—to name just three examples—in one country have aided planning for the present and the future in another. Planning which rests in part on this particular base is obviously not possible without comparison.

Comparative studies in published form will foster the free exchange of ideas, upon which exchange the vitality and the advancement of all fields to a very large extent depend.

One may suggest also, if somewhat hesitantly, that comparative studies in a social field like ours may serve to foster and improve international understanding, not only through the dissemination of published works, but also through the personal contacts—correspondence, visits, discussions, and so on—which are generally necessary for their creation.

Comparative studies may also contribute, in a way that no others can, to the solution of a library problem, particularly one with international implications. An example is the commonly recognized need for more or less universally accepted cataloging practices, which resulted in the critical analysis of national practices at the International Conference on Cataloguing Principles, 1961, and, eventually, the international *Statement of Principles*.[25] Another example is the activity which produced the *International Standard Bibliographic Description* (London: IFLA, 1971).

Since the end of the Second World War, librarians from many of the advanced countries have been increasingly involved in consultation, surveys, study visits, and work assignments in countries other than their own. Comparative studies, even of library systems and practices in countries other than those where the student or consultant expects to be, may be of benefit to him from a methodological or procedural point of view; if the studies concern "his" country or countries, and thus include specific background information about them, so much the better.

Far too little attention has been paid in library education programs everywhere to the potential value of comparative studies in strengthening such programs and increasing their scholarly content (Collings's point 6). With the exception of a very few areas, chiefly cataloging, classification, and bibliography, the student in the typical one- or two-year library education program

[25] Eva Verona et al., *Statement of Principles Adopted at the International Conference on Cataloguing Principles, Paris, October, 1961*. Annotated edition with commentary and examples (London: IFLA Committee on Cataloguing [British Museum], 1971).

is seldom exposed to practices and procedures except those common or dominant in the country or region where he studies. Even in these areas, at the beginning level of library education it is probably fair to say that few students outside of Great Britain, the British Commonwealth, and North America ever hear of Ranganathan, and few outside of Great Britain and North America ever learn of Bliss. It is not that students need to "know" such "different" classifications as these, but, rather, that they should be made aware of the differing *principles* upon which the classification systems rest. When it comes to matters such as developments in library architecture; the central public library services of the Scandinavian countries; the issue of broad versus close book classification; regional union catalogs; large-scale open-shelf university library book collections; intensive professional reference service; and many, many others, the evidence we have suggests that the "beginning" library school student learns little or nothing of them unless they are common in the country where he studies. He would be a more aware librarian, and one more able to weigh and judge alternatives, if he did.

In connection with several of the foregoing points, the ideas of a French legal comparativist, René David, are worth noting:

> To enclose legal science within the boundaries of one nation, and to pretend to explain or develop it without taking into account foreign thought and experience, is to limit both the possibilities of knowledge and the sphere of action of the jurist. No more than history, economics, political science or sociology, can law—a social science—be properly studied from a purely national point of view. Juridical nationalism is provincialism, and irreconcilable with a truly scientific spirit; it impoverishes and indeed is dangerous to the development and even the application of a national law.[26]

[26] René David, *Major Legal Systems in the World Today: An Introduction to the Comparative Study of Law*, trans. John E. C. Brierley (London: Stevens, 1968), p. 8.

Precisely the same may be said, with almost equal force, about librarianship.

The author goes on to note that not all of those who are to become legal practitioners need receive an education in comparative law, and that the study of any national law is generally sufficient for those who simply want to acquire a technical training. For those who wish a general legal culture, however, comparative law, like history of law, is a necessity.[27] This view, also, is fully applicable to librarianship.

At the advanced, or doctoral/research level, some students certainly become acquainted with the international and comparative, but such students represent only a minute fraction of our total output, and it is a still smaller fraction of these advanced students who participate in comparative work. A review, for example, of the more than four hundred doctoral dissertations in librarianship thus far produced in the United States, reveals that fewer than five percent of them have a comparative or international content.

Another purpose of comparative as, indeed, of all other kinds of intellectual studies, is that of increasing the sum total of our knowledge, the purpose, that is, of advancing its frontiers, and of doing so solely for the sake of the knowledge to be gained. Many academicians would claim that this purpose is, if not the only real justification for scholarly inquiry, at least the main one, and would call such studies "pure research," or "pure comparative librarianship." They would have considerable grounds for their claim, and could point to the fact that many of the world's most significant discoveries have come about simply because a man was somehow inspired to learn something not previously known. Proponents of the position could also note that in many of our leading universities the support, encouragement, and ap-

[27] Ibid., pp. 8–9.

preciation of creative effort is in direct relationship to its abstract and theoretical nature, whereas the highly practical or "applied" and purposeful inquiry tends to be viewed in a less favorable light. The writer would be inclined to support the *scientia gratis scientiae* view, and submits that a cardinal justification for comparative librarianship is intellectual; knowledge for its own sake would be sufficient ground for our serious concern with it, even if none other existed. But whatever position the reader takes, the fact is that we probably do not have a dozen solid works which are entitled to the appellation "pure comparative librarianship."

Two related general benefits of comparative studies or, perhaps more precisely, of the comparative method, almost never discussed in our literature, may be mentioned. They may be introduced by asking a question: why should we analyze cross-cultural or cross-national data at all? Would it not be better, as it is certainly in many respects easier, to limit ourselves to materials acquired in our own society or culture, where language, tradition, the sociological milieu, and history are familiar to us and where, further, better control of the nature and collection of data is probably possible? The answers, that is, the positive values or benefits of the cross-societal study are two. In the first place, it provides the possibility that the generalizations we seek to establish, and the results of our testing of hypotheses, are applicable beyond the confines of a single culture. Studies made in the United States have generally shown, for instance, that there is a strong positive correlation between the amount of public library use and geographical proximity of library facilities to the user. Does this hold true, as well, in other, quite different societies with possibly different attitudes toward the "taking of time and trouble?"

In short, such generalizations and principles as we may derive from studying a problem, situation, or condition have *ipso facto* only limited demonstrable applicability and validity if the study is confined to a single country. One may go still further and note, again, that some kinds of investigation, such as the study or reconciliation of national or regional cataloging codes, cannot be pursued at all except on a comparative basis.

The second and related advantage is that the more different kinds of societies examined, the greater the range of many of the variables is likely to be.

An illustration of this, and of the resulting benefit, may be submitted by considering two countries, one of which is large, undeveloped, predominantly rural; the second, small, developed, and heavily settled. The first country has few public libraries, and it takes the inhabitants, on the average, about two hours to reach the nearest one. In the second country, with a wide-spread public library system, the inhabitants are, on the average, fifteen minutes distant from the nearest service. In the second (developed) country, there is a high correlation between proximity to public library service and use of it, whereas in the first (undeveloped) country the correlation is very low; in other words, as distance from libraries increases in the second country, use decreases, whereas this decrease is very slight in the first country.

In a comparative study involving the two countries, the range of the variable, "average distance in time from the nearest public library service," is far greater than would be the case if the study were limited to the second country alone. Since, despite the greater average distance, the proportion of inhabitants in the first country seeking public library service is about as great as in the second, compelling reasons would need to account for the fact. For example, it might be found that time, and the many commitments which reduce its availability, was a relatively unimportant consideration in the case of the first country, whose inhabitants, therefore, had no hesitation in taking the necessary time and trouble to reach a library. Or, it might be discovered that, whereas in the second country, the inhabitants have ready access to numerous other sources of information such as newspapers, magazines, radio, community film and lecture programs, television, and bookstores, in the first country none of these sources is readily available. Both factors—or some other —might, of course, account for the observed difference.

4

The Dimensions of Publication, Research and Education

It was suggested in the Introduction that librarianship, though it has accomplished much of great value at the international level, has produced very little in the way of real comparative work. Some writers have stated or implied a contrary view. "Until very recently," Chase Dane has written,

> there has not existed the requisite volume of professional literature to enable anyone to embark on [comparative librarianship studies]. There has now, however, within the last ten or twenty years, grown up a respectable body of professional literature which can be studied from a comparative point of view with profit.
>
> One has only to examine the leading professional journals of four or five countries to see that this is true. Keeping within the confines of the English language one reads with increasing respect periodical library literature of the United States, Canada, Australia, South Africa, New Zealand, and India. After one has read even the most important articles

83

in the recent library journals of these countries, one begins to realize how impressive is becoming the body of library literature in the English language alone.[1]

This statement was contrary to fact when Dane wrote it, and it is contrary to fact today.

Although a great deal has been written on the two subjects, one could not, for instance, make a satisfactory comparative study of "foreign" library education programs or of European university libraries on the basis of the articles about them that appeared in volume 12 of *Library Trends* (Oct. 1963 and Apr. 1964). The authors of the several articles begin with varying assumptions and purposes, include different sorts of data that are neither complete nor comparable, and use varying terminology, often imprecise or, at best, different from that used by other authors. In short, a valid and defensible comparison simply cannot be made. The same is true almost everywhere one looks at our published literature.

Jean Hassenforder suggests that, in the public library field, at least, "we can draw on a relative abundance of information and notably detailed descriptions."[2]

Dorothy Collings and Sylvia Simsova, also, strongly imply that we now have a substantial number of comparative studies and a body of literature from which satisfactory studies can readily be produced.[3] In fact, we do not.

Notably lacking, too, as demonstrated in chapter 2, are studies of a theoretical nature which satisfactorily define our terminology and defensibly and logically describe our scope and meth-

[1] Chase Dane, "The Benefits of Comparative Librarianship," *The Australian Library Journal*, 3:89 (July 1954).

[2] Jean Hassenforder, "Comparative Studies and the Development of Public Libraries," *UNESCO Bulletin for Libraries* 22:15 (Jan.-Feb. 1968).

[3] S. Simsova and M. MacKee, *A Handbook of Comparative Librarianship* (London: Bingley, c1970), pp. 7, 57–370; Dorothy Collings, "Comparative Librarianship," in *Encyclopedia of Library and Information Science*, 5:492.

odology, as, for example, Isaac Kandel's *Comparative Education*, Harold J. Noah and Max Eckstein's *Toward a Science of Comparative Education*, and Friedrich Schneider's *Vergleichende Erziehungswissenschaft* do for education. The literature we have was reviewed in chapters 2 and 3 and is listed in the Bibliography at the end of the volume.

A third and final major lack is that of comparative studies themselves—studies, that is, which are at the same time genuinely comparative and cross-societal, as defined in chapter 2, and have been conducted on the basis of minimum standards of scholarly investigation.

Lest there be misunderstanding about the point being made here, it may be noted that our literature, especially since World War II, includes scores of monographs, surveys, and reports, and hundreds of articles about libraries or aspects of librarianship in various countries—what Collings, Simsova, and others define as case or area studies. Much of this writing is descriptive and narrative, often subjective and didactic, usually entirely innocent of sound methodology, and, in the overwhelming majority of cases, *not comparative at all*. Such writing, involving the gathering, with little or no interpretation, of direct information about developments, trends, or status of libraries, or some aspect of librarianship in "another" country (*Auslandskunde*, or "foreign librarianship"), is typified by the article having a title which reads, "The University Libraries of ——: Report of a Study Tour," or "The Public Libraries of Great Britain," or "Austria: Its Libraries and Librarianship." As noted in chapter 2 such studies cannot be called comparative, anymore than the study of a language by one whose native tongue is another language could be called comparative linguistics. The nationality of the author, is, in fact, immaterial; writing limited to a single country, society, or culture is simply not comparative.

But one must go further than this. The issue is not solely, or even primarily, that study limited to a single society is not comparative. In librarianship thus far, even most work involving two or more societies cannot properly be described as comparative. The issue, accordingly, is a fundamental one, and broader than might at first appear. It is considered in detail in the following chapter, but the essential argument needs to be noted here. This argument is, simply, that the mere compilation and presentation of data about the library situation in a number of societies, no matter how exhaustive and carefully done the compilation may be, does not constitute comparison. Kandel makes the point for education in saying that descriptions of foreign school systems in terms of buildings, teacher salaries, pupil distribution, and methods of instruction, and articles on the educational systems of different countries, remain simply descriptions, and do not themselves constitute comparative studies.[4] Even when such descriptions include analyses, as he later notes, and thus may serve to contribute to comparative study, they cannot, themselves, justifiably be described by the word comparative.[5] Almost every writer in the social sciences who has considered this matter has made the same point.[6]

In short, "comparative" means just what it says, namely, that differences and similarities must be placed in direct juxtaposition with one another, and the differences must be explained in terms of all relevant aspects of the social milieu. It is not information *about* library phenomena in different societies which constitutes comparative study but, rather, inquiry *into* the phenomena and the conditions and factors which have determined their nature and have accounted for differences between them.

Two further observations should be made here. The first is that if descriptive studies of the kind mentioned in the preced-

---

[4] Issac L. Kandel, *The New Era in Education: A Comparative Study* (New York: Houghton Mifflin, c1955), p. 6.

[5] Ibid., pp. 8–9.

[6] See, for example, Harold J. Noah and Max A. Eckstein, *Toward a Science of Comparative Education* (New York: Macmillan, 1969), pp. 187–88; and Franz Hilker, *Vergleichende Pädagogik* (Munich: Hueber, 1962), p. 65.

ing paragraphs are well done—that is, if the data they report are accurate, full, and carefully analyzed—they will be highly useful, and the fact that the studies are not in any sense comparative is not in itself ground for criticism. Unhappily, relatively little of our published literature meets even these criteria. The second point is that a contribution, the title of which reads "French and Italian Public Libraries: Views from a Busman's Holiday," while clearly "comparative" in the sense of having a cross-national element, is very likely not a good comparative study.

Some demonstration and substantiation of the foregoing criticism of our internationally oriented literature seems called for. Consequently, the paragraphs which follow consider a number of generally well-known monographs which have been called— though not always by their authors—comparative studies. These publications have been selected because first, they all, with a single exception, have a multi-national content or approach, and, second, they are all, in one way or another, valuable and useful contributions to our literature. Indeed, the present writer has published favorable reviews of some of them. The point being considered, therefore, has nothing to do with the quality of these publications, but, rather, whether they are good *comparative* studies—or, in fact, comparative studies at all.

One can begin with an early work, a near classic and unique publication, commonly and favorably included in our comparative literature: Wilhelm Munthe's *American Librarianship from a European Angle* (Chicago: American Library Assn., 1939; repr. Hamden, Conn.: Shoe String Pr., 1969).[7] On the personal invitation of Frederick P. Keppel, president, Carnegie Corporation of New York, Munthe, the able and experienced director of the National and University Library in Oslo, spent three months in the United States and Canada, visiting and observing various aspects of the North American library scene. The result of his

[7] Cf., e.g., D. J. Foskett, "Comparative Librarianship," in Robert L. Collison, ed., *Progress in Library Science, 1965* (London: Butterworths, 1965), p. 129; S. Simsova and M. MacKee, *Handbook,* p. 28.

observations and reflections was a penetrating critique, which put its finger upon many weak spots of American library practice, and was not without some effect upon it. The work still provides interesting and profitable reading. Nonetheless, it is not a good comparative study. For one thing, real comparison is almost wholly lacking, in that only by inference is the reader able to divine that the practices and conditions which Munthe criticizes are opposite to those of (presumably) Norway or Europe. In short, the Norwegian or European side of the comparison is seldom made explicitly and precisely clear. Further, *American Librarianship* is a highly impressionistic and subjective work, for frequently categorical statements are made for which almost no real "evidence" is offered. There is no clear statement of hypothesis, no testing of the unstated hypotheses, no scientific proof of the contentions made, and no way that the reader himself can verify, on the basis of what is offered, these claims and contentions.

Another and even earlier publication is Arthur Elmore Bostwick's *Popular Libraries of the World* (Chicago: American Library Assn., 1933), published in connection with the Chicago meeting of the International Federation of Library Associations in that year.[8] Bostwick and the ALA invited knowledgeable persons from more than seventy countries which at the time had, or were thought to have, popular or public libraries, to write contributions about them. Altogether, forty-eight countries are represented in the volume. The coverage, therefore, is clearly international. But the work is in no sense a comparative one, for no comparisons of any kind are made, or even attempted. Further, useful comparisons could not, in fact, be drawn from the contributions because their authors have widely differing approaches, do not present the same kinds or amounts of data, and frequently use different terminology in their descriptions.

Another publication in the international field, provocative and stimulating like Munthe's, and commonly considered a

[8] Cf. Simsova and MacKee, *Handbook*, p. 28.

comparative work, is Lester Asheim's *Librarianship in the Developing Countries.*[9] Like Munthe's work, Asheim's is the product of a shrewd and experienced observer. The author analyzes and draws conclusions from data (i.e., observations) known, for the most part, only to him and therefore not verifiable by the reader. The lectures can only barely be called comparative in that a precise matching or contrasting of conditions and practices in two different countries or cultures is seldom present or possible.

In one of his contributions to a volume he edited on librarianship in Britain, Canada, Denmark, the Federal Republic of Germany, and the United States, Carl M. White proposes to use the method of comparative librarianship "to identify some of the common characteristics, or tendencies, which emerge from empirical study" of the papers on Britain, Germany, and the United States.[10] In the broadest terms, White achieves this purpose, but a great deal of what he offers as fact and conclusion in this paper is directly derivable form his own broad knowledge and experience, rather than from the evidence supplied by the six contributions on the three named countries. Further, the papers are so different from each other, particularly in the nature and amount of data supplied, that direct comparisons and conclusions, in a comparative sense, are not possible except in extremely broad terms, such as, an objective of the library programs of the countries is "to aid formal instruction," or "to further research."

The series in which John Ferguson's *Libraries in France* (Hamden, Conn.: Shoe String Pr., 1971) appeared is called Comparative Library Studies, and the volume is described as a comparative study. *Libraries in France* includes a great deal of useful, factual information about the French library system in

[9] Cf., e.g., Collings, "Comparative Librarianship," p. 500.

[10] Carl M. White, "Comparative Study of Library Systems," in Carl M. White, ed., *Bases of Modern Librarianship* (Oxford: Pergamon Pr., 1964), p. 13.

general and about all of the important, and many not so important, libraries of the country. It is, therefore, a most useful reference tool, or *vade mecum* for a librarian on a trip to France.
Nothing whatever in the volume is in the slightest degree comparative—or intended to be; *Libraries in France* is, in fact, no
more a "comparative work" than is the *American Library Directory* or the *Jahrbuch der Deutschen Bibliotheken*.

Arundell Esdaile's widely known and used volume, *National
Libraries of the World* . . . (2nd ed., revised by F. J. Hill; London: Library Assn., 1957) is, in scope, like Bostwick's, about
as international as a work can be, and it is frequently pointed
to as a major study in comparative librarianship. The work is the
only one of the kind that we have and, in its provision of detailed history, sources of funds, principal collections, and so on,
of all the important national libraries of the world, it is enormously useful even though now considerably out of date. It is
not, however, a "major study" in comparative librarianship. On
the contrary, it is a solely factual description and narration,
wholly lacking in direct comparison or any attempt at interpretation and explanation.

The extent to which the work is not comparative is further
illustrated by the fact that the data included are not the same
for any two institutions. Sometimes salary figures, number of
staff, amount of annual income (or expenditure), total number
of volumes, annual accessions, and number of readers are given;
sometimes they are not; and when they are given, definitions
of what constitutes "readers," for instance, are not offered. In
short, a meaningful comparative study could not be made on
the basis of the several accounts included in the volume.

K. C. Harrison's deservedly praised and highly useful volume
on Scandinavian libraries is a good study, but it is not a *comparative* study.[11] Almost nothing in the way of direct comparison
between the Scandinavian countries themselves, or these and
other countries, is provided; any such comparisons which it is

---

[11] K. C. Harrison, *Libraries in Scandinavia* (London: Deutsch, 1961).

possible to make, the reader must make for himself. There is almost no attempt to provide explanation, in any terms what-ever—either economic, sociological, political, or educational—of the facts and situations presented. Finally, Harrison does not, except briefly in a two-and-a-half-page concluding chapter, pre-sent any synthesis of his material, and there is certainly no at-tempt at providing principles or a theoretical base. In short, despite the wealth of valuable information which has been care-fully brought together and clearly and logically presented, the study is simply a straight-forward narrative and descriptive ac-count, which stops precisely at the point where real comparative investigation begins.[12] This same statement applies to a very great deal of our internationally oriented literature.

It could be made, for another instance, with very little quali-fication, of H. C. Campbell's book on large municipal public libraries.[13] Campbell points out in his Introduction that "most of the material in this book is descriptive" and that "attempts have been made only occasionally to compare one metropolitan area with another."[14] The point is illustrated by the fact that only one of the twenty-four tables includes data for more than a single city or country, and this table has to do simply with urban population growth. Explanation, also, is minimal, and,

[12] Foskett offers a diametrically opposed judgment: "It is interesting to see, in this book, how the comparative approach develops out of what began as a series of case studies. [Not so.] Harrison notes methods that are peculiar to one country, or shared by several countries with significant modi-fications from one to another. [True.] While analysing the reasons for these he is led to discuss the historical and sociological influences that have pro-duced them, and to suggest some ways in which British librarians might profitably follow the Scandinavian example." (A careful reading of Harri-son justifies the last part of this sentence only.) D. J. Foskett, "Compara-tive Librarianship," in Robert L. Collison, ed., Progress in Library Science, 1965 (London: Butterworths, 1965), p. 130.

[13] H. C. Campbell, Metropolitan Public Library Planning Throughout the World (Oxford: Pergamon Pr., c1967). Cf. Simsova and MacKee, Handbook, p. 26.

[14] Campbell, Metropolitan Public Library Planning, p. x.

when offered, is seldom clearly or directly relatable to the data. The same may be said of the generalizations which appear in the first three and last chapters.

As a final illustration, William Vernon Jackson's well-known and highly useful work on Latin-American librarianship may be cited.[15] Jackson is one of the few real experts on the subject outside of Latin America itself, and his is still the most comprehensive account in English. The author pays at least some attention to some aspects of librarianship in each of the twenty Latin American countries, and he provides a number of interesting generalizations regarding, for instance, their national, university, and public libraries, and education for librarianship. For the most part, however, these generalizations are not directly derivable from the data included, very few data are carried through from country to country, and most of what is offered by way of conclusion and "principle" stems from the author's great knowledge and experience, rather than from data available to the reader. This is not, then, a comparative study, as Jackson would probably be the first to admit.

The foregoing critiques could readily be multiplied a hundredfold, but no useful purpose would be served by adding to the list.

It may be argued that these critiques take too narrow a view. It may be claimed, as is in most instances the case, that the studies were not intended to be "real" comparative studies, that they are good and useful works, which is also true, and that we should let it go at that. Good and useful for what? Useful for the individual who wants carefully compiled and accurate information about something? Yes, generally. Useful for one who wishes a running, narrative account of something? Yes, often. Useful as providing some kind of information about some aspects of librarianship in certain countries? Yes. But useful as a means to help us really understand the causes of observed phe-

[15] William Vernon Jackson, *Aspects of Librarianship in Latin America* (Champaign, Ill.: distributed by the Illini Bookstore, 1962).

nomena, or to assist us in establishing principles which underlie some of them—useful, therefore in the sense of advancing
the profession in fundamental ways? No.

Under the rubric "comparative librarianship," *Library and
Information Science Abstracts* (*LISA*) for the five-year period,
1966–70, indexes fifty-nine articles, reports, surveys, and other
publications. A review of these (judgment concerning five writings in Eastern European and Oriental languages based upon
abstracts only) reveals that thirteen are concerned with a single
country; they are not, therefore, in any sense comparative, and
LISA might more appropriately have entered them under the
heading "international librarianship." Of the forty-six remain-
ing items, seventeen are impressions of visits and study tours;
nine (all cited in chapter 2 or 3) are about comparative or international librarianship, and four are reports of conferences. All
of the other sixteen pieces are definitely cross-societal, but only
four contain elements of real comparison; two of these are serious comparative studies. The overwhelming majority of all of
the writings are between two and seven pages in length. The
hard and inescapable fact is that a solid, comparative study of
the libraries of two countries, or even of library education, or
the public or university libraries of two countries, cannot be
encompassed in such short space.

It should come as no surprise whatever, therefore, that a distinguished scholar, in reviewing the status and contributions
of comparative studies in this century, makes no reference at
all to work in librarianship.[16]

In partial summary of the foregoing, then, it may be said that
the overwhelming majority of the large body of "international"
and "comparative" literature in librarianship consists either of

1. Narrative, descriptive accounts of particular situations
   ("Public Libraries in Germany Today")

[16] Edward Shils, "Seeing It Whole," *Times Literary Supplement* (London), 28 July 1966, pp. 647–48.

2. Opinions, usually offered with little or no supporting evidence ("A Danish View of Library Education in the Middle East" or "Observations from a Study Tour of University Libraries in Asia")
3. Bodies of data, often accurate and reasonably comprehensive, on some aspect(s) of some kinds of libraries ("Bookstock, Annual Acquisitions, and Annual Budgets of the National Libraries of Western Europe")
4. Surveys, reports, and the like ("Report to UNESCO on the Need for a Library Education Program in——").

Most of these are interesting, many have practical, highly important value, and some are useful for comparative study. But few are cross-societal and fewer still state or test a hypothesis, provide careful analysis of data, attempt to provide explanation or generalization or are truly comparative.

It seems possible to suggest several reasons for the lack of development of comparative studies in librarianship.

During that part of the nineteenth century when numerous other disciplines were being stimulated by the results of the application of scientific methods in biology and linguistics, librarianship was a completely pragmatic pursuit and nowhere recognized as a field of academic or even serious study. It received no academic recognition whatever until the founding of the School of Library Service at Columbia University in 1887, and even then, and for the next forty years, instruction in the United States remained on a practical, mostly elementary level. The first schools in Germany and England were not founded until 1905 and 1919, respectively. Nothing even approaching research was being conducted anywhere, except for some bibliographical and historical work, chiefly in Europe. The field simply was not ready for anything different.

Most disciplines, however, are primarily advanced through the teaching and research carried on at universities, and a review of the important figures in comparative studies in anthropology, education, government, linguistics, sociology, and so on reveals that the great majority of the authors were, or are, at least in some fashion, academicians, and that most were, or are, members of university faculties. The embryonic state of comparative librarianship may in large part be explained by the fact that relatively few schools of librarianship have embraced comparative study in their programs; still fewer have treated it as a major and important part of their whole effort; none has been concerned with the area extensively or for long; and none has mounted a significant research program.

Among the institutions that pay some attention to it are the College of Librarianship at Aberystwyth; the *Institut für Bibliothekswissenschaft und Wissenschaftliche Information*, Humboldt University, Berlin; the School of Library Service, Columbia University; the Department of Librarianship, the Polytechnic of Leeds; the School of Librarianship, Polytechnic of North London; the Graduate School of Library and Information Science, Pratt Institute; Graduate School of Library Service, Rutgers University; School of Library Science, Simmons College; the State Library School at Copenhagen; the School of Library Science, State University College, Geneseo, New York; the School of Librarianship and Archives, University College, London; and the schools at the universities of California (Berkeley), Chicago, Ibadan, Illinois, Indiana, Pittsburgh, Sheffield, Syracuse, Texas, Toronto, Washington, and Wisconsin. More than a score of other schools in Canada and the United States also give at least some attention to the subject.

There are three interesting points about this list. One is the absence from it of the several strong library schools of West Germany and the Soviet Union, and the two strong schools of Czechoslovakia. (Some research is being conducted at the Lenin Library, which publishes *Bibliotekovedenie za rubezhom* [*Librarianship Abroad*].)

Some work in comparative librarianship is certainly being done even in library education agencies that offer no courses in the subject and do not otherwise formally include it in their programs. A case in point is the Chair of Librarianship and Information Science (*Katedra Knihovnictví A Vědeckých Informaci*) of Charles University, Prague, a library school perhaps less well known to most readers of these lines than many others. One of the requirements for completion of its basic five-year program is a paper at about the level of a master's thesis in the United States. Of the approximately five hundred such works thus far submitted for the diploma, eight are comparative studies. As examples, one of these compares the social status of the librarian in France, the East German Democratic Republic, Sweden, the United States, the USSR, and Yugoslavia; another deals with library networks in Prague and Warsaw; and a third treats, comparatively, information systems in Czechoslovakia and the USSR. Some members of the faculty have also undertaken, under a general "state information policy" investigation, a study of the education of information and library workers in selected countries. This study covers such matters as course characteristics and objectives, admission requirements, curriculum analysis, and program length.

Similarly, of the 385 studies (*Hausarbeiten*) submitted in partial fulfilment of the requirements for the higher service in scholarly libraries (*Höheren Dienst an wissenschaftlichen Bibliotheken*) at Cologne, half a dozen, judged by their titles, are to some degree comparative works.[17] No doubt much the same kind of statement could be made for some other library education agencies which have a thesis or thesis-like requirement for the completion of their programs.

It is surprising that West Germany, which has made such signal contributions to comparative study, not least in education, has produced insignificantly in librarianship, either from library education or outside it, and has ignored comparative

[17] Ingeborg Konze and Ludwig Sickmann, *Verzeichnis der beim Bibliothekar-Lehrinstitut des Landes Nordrhein-Westfalen 1949–1970 angefertigten Hausarbeiten für den Höheren Dienst an Wissenschaftlichen Bibliotheken.* Bibliothekar-Lehrinstitut des Landes Nordrhein-Westfalen, Bibliographische Hefte no. 6. (Cologne: Greven Verlag, 1971).

work entirely in its library education curricula. A possible reason may be the fact that library education agencies in that country have no university connection and therefore lack the stimulus and fructification which a relationship with other disciplines might supply. The universities of Hamburg and Munich, the UNESCO Institute for Education at Hamburg, and the *Hochschule für Internationale Pädagogische Forschung* in Frankfurt, are very strong centers of comparative education, and there are major library schools in all three cities.

A more telling point about the list is that virtually all of the library schools which have the most extensive and elaborate programs in comparative studies—such as the ones at the College of Librarianship, Aberystwyth, the Polytechnic of North London (with the equivalent of one full-time comparativist faculty member), and Pratt Institute—have only introductory work in the field, have no research programs, staff, or funds for them and often have high staff teaching loads, which, even in the absence of other deterrents, would make major research activity almost impossible. At the British polytechnics, for instance, the teaching load may be as high as eighteen class hours a week.

The reverse is that the schools with a major commitment to research, through doctoral or other programs, with access to research funds, and with low faculty teaching loads, are precisely those that have given only a minimal, left-handed kind of attention to comparative librarianship. Typically, they offer only a course or two through a regular or part-time member of the staff, most of whose time and energy are devoted elsewhere. Examples of these institutions are the University of California (Berkeley), the University of Chicago, Columbia University, the University of Illinois, Indiana University, University College (London), the University of Sheffield, and the University of Wisconsin. Most of them, it may be noted, are particularly strong in area, "foreign," and comparative studies in other disciplines.

97

A comprehensive survey of the accredited library schools in Canada and the United States revealed that "the majority of the schools (85 per cent or seventeen of the twenty) which give curriculum lip-service to international and comparative librarianship do so through an introductory course, or a unit of another course; the number of schools which carry this further via more intensive study . . . is quite small."[18] Later, the author makes this statement more specific by saying that only four schools "offer more than one course in the international field."[19]

While the latest directory of American library schools reports that some forty-five institutions—a considerable increase over the twenty of 1968—apparently offer at least one course in comparative (or international) librarianship, the catalogs and announcements of these schools still show that fewer than half a dozen do anything beyond a single introductory course or two.

In 1959 the Ford Foundation, at the request of the United States Department of State, created a committee charged with the definition of the role of the American university in world affairs. Six of the committee's sixteen recommendations are addressed to universities and colleges, and the second of the six is:

> All American universities should improve the competence of their graduate and professional schools to teach and to conduct research on international aspects of their disciplines and professions.[20]

[18] Beverly J. Brewster, "International Library School Programs," *Journal of Education for Librarianship* 9:139 (Fall 1968).

[19] Ibid., p. 141.

[20] Ford Foundation, Committee on the University and World Affairs, *The University and World Affairs* (New York: The Foundation, 1960), p. 4.

In elaboration, the committee writes:

> A heavy burden rests on graduate and professional schools to strengthen the international components of their regular departments, interdepartmental programs and centers, scholarship in languages and linguistics, and library and other material resources. Most of those who will become teachers or international specialists in other careers are trained in such schools.[21]

The committee further notes that:

> The educational focus of most professional schools in American universities is overwhelmingly domestic for the strong vocational reason that they train students to practice professions in the United States, and frequently in specific states. In important ways, this principle of professional education has been outmoded by the growing American involvement with the rest of the world. A significant proportion of professional graduates can expect to find part of their careers in foreign areas, whether their profession be law, education, public administration, business, medicine, public health, engineering, or agriculture. If only on this utilitarian ground, the case is clear for an effective international component in the programs of the stronger professional schools. The case also rests on the wider grounds that American professions have a responsibility for the international aspects of their fields, that they need to understand other societies if they are to understand our own, and that many of the major problems of their fields are also found in other societies.[22]

Since the publication of this report, as earlier noted, the number of library schools in the United States (and Canada) that pay some attention to the international and comparative aspects of librarianship has substantially increased (from five in

[21] Ibid., p. 20.
[22] Ibid., pp. 23–24.

1963 to forty-five in 1972), and this is certainly a considerable step forward. But, as also noted, "an effective international component" is hardly to be found anywhere in the programs of our schools, either in the United States or Europe, and especially not in the programs "of the stronger professional schools."

In 1956, Walter Crosby Eells published a study of doctoral dissertations in North American universities. Among his findings was that, of more than 15,000 dissertations in the field of education, about 8 percent, or approximately 1,200 were concerned with education in "foreign" countries.[23] Clearly not all of these were comparative studies, but a large number of them were. Librarianship, two decades later, has produced scarcely a dozen.

To be quite specific, we do not have in any library education agency anywhere a thorough-going, full-fledged program to assure the student who wishes to become a comparativist that he will—through courses, seminars, and tutorials—acquire:

1. A knowledge of general research method and of the methodology and techniques of comparative study and research
2. An extensive and intensive knowledge of librarianship in some other countries
3. The capacity to analyze, judge critically, and use "foreign" sources
4. A knowledge of the history, methods, and meaning of comparative librarianship in general
5. An objective, scholarly attitude and a critical judgment of the findings of comparative studies, particularly in librarianship
6. Command of (some) foreign languages, a topic discussed below.

A suggested outline of a course or seminar covering the strictly "comparative librarianship" parts of the above is given in the Appendix.

[23] Walter Crosby Eells, "Dissertations on Foreign Education Accepted by American Universities," *The Journal of Educational Sociology* 3:147–56 (Nov. 1956).

The student in the doctoral or research program in the stronger library education agencies in the United States and abroad receives some of this, particularly knowledge of general research method and, it is hoped, a scholarly and critical point of view. At those institutions where some attention is paid to comparative librarianship, he will get something more, and more specific, than this. But, to repeat, nowhere can he get all that he should.

The foregoing comments—like the critiques of some of our published literature, and like the discussion of area studies and *Auslandskunde* in chapter 2—are not in the slightest degree intended to undervalue teaching of comparative librarianship at an elementary level. We need much more of such teaching, just as we need more good area studies, and it seems unlikely that we shall advance very far or very fast in genuine comparative work until we have more. That is, it is improbable that we shall develop a corps of producing scholars until more students have been introduced to the subject at the elementary level. An important point in all of this is that many kinds of work and documentation, along with teaching at the beginning level, belong to the *subject* of comparative librarianship, but that this is not the same as, though it is related to, research and research productivity in comparative librarianship.

All this, of course, is not to say that advancement will come only through the universities, or that important contributions will not sometimes be made by persons outside them. But the evidence is, in comparative studies in librarianship as elsewhere, that these will today be the exceptions. The practicing librarian has a position, the successful prosecution of which takes about all of the time and energy he has. He is employed to perform a certain task for a library, and not to undertake research or investigation. He has no particular incentive to do so on his own, and will generally be little rewarded if he does. He is typically not research oriented or research trained. The exact opposite is, or should be, the case with a member of the faculty of a university: he has the time, the commitment, the incentive, the training, and some access to needed funds and research assistance. It seems inevitable, therefore, that if we are to seek major improvement in our situation, we must look for it in the library education agencies having strong doctoral programs and/or research commitments and capabilities.

Another reason for our present situation, and a reason no doubt at least partially related to the foregoing, is the paucity of qualified personnel. No work in the social fields places higher demands upon those who pursue it than do comparative studies. At their best, satisfactory teaching and, especially, research call for some command of foreign languages and cultures; a sound knowledge of library history and of at least some particular aspects of libraries and librarianship; a knowledge of research methodology in the social fields; an insight into the intellectual, ideological, and sociological forces which have produced the world, or some parts of the world we know today; and probably—as comparative librarianship largely concerns the present day—substantial foreign travel in some parts of the world. Very few librarians, in or out of universities, possess all of these desiderata.

The inclusion in this listing of foreign travel and knowledge of languages may be questioned by some, and it is certainly true that many librarians, particularly Anglo-Americans, have attempted studies of countries other than their own without a knowledge of the languages of those countries, and occasionally, without visiting them. It is difficult, however, to name a good study in comparative librarianship in which this has been the case. Most investigators in other disciplines, with far more (and more successful) experience than we, who have expressed themselves on the point, leave no doubt as to their views. It has been the writer's own experience, also, that studying a library matter in situ and discussing it with a foreign colleague in his own language are almost essential, and certainly have enormous benefits. To work through an interpreter, or to discuss a problem with someone in a language not his own, or to examine a problem wholly on the basis of documentation almost always leads to errors of fact and interpretation. Our literature is replete with examples. George Bereday makes a very strong case both for language and foreign travel and, in fact, devotes two of his twelve chapters to them.[24] In another place he cites his experience with a study in Colombia. He describes at some length the data and information he gleaned from existing printed sources before his trip and then shows how, in the light of what he observed and learned after arriving in Colombia, the picture presented by the literature was revealed to be false at almost every point.[25]

A detailed and documented case for language knowledge and for travel, particularly for extensive stay in the countries the comparativist proposes to study, is also made by Friedrich Schneider.[26] The importance of travel and a knowledge of foreign languages is likewise stressed by Kandel, Brickman, Joachim Wach, and Hilker, among others.[27]

A final likely cause of the present situation is the indifference, verging on downright antagonism, which comparative studies often meet. The Anglo-American library world, which has led the profession in so many notable respects—as, for example, in the development of work with children; the idea of wholly free public library service, open to all; library extension; centralized

[24] George Z. F. Bereday, *Comparative Method in Education* (New York: Holt, c1964).

[25] George Z. F. Bereday, "A Colombian Lesson in Comparative Method," *Teachers College Record* 58, no. 7:355–63 (1956–57).

[26] Friedrich Schneider, *Vergleichende Erziehungswissenschaft* (Heidelberg: Quelle and Meyer, 1961), pp. 136–42.

[27] Isaac L. Kandel, "The Methodology of Comparative Education," *International Review of Education* 5:278 (1959); William W. Brickman, "Comparative Education," in *Encyclopedia of Educational Research* (1969), p. 184; Joachim Wach, *The Comparative Study of Religions* (New York: Columbia Univ. Pr., 1958); Franz Hilker, *Vergleichende Pädagogik*, pp. 107–9.

administration of university libraries; the development of cataloging codes, automation, and so on—has been particularly guilty here. The "typical" Anglo-American librarian is deplorably ignorant of much of what is happening elsewhere in the library world; so far as the European continent is concerned, the language barrier may provide one explanation. At any rate, there often seems to be a subconscious fear that our own traditional methods may be disrupted, or even somehow damaged, by the introduction of ideas resulting from inquiry into what is going on elsewhere. Although we may not necessarily claim that our procedures and practices are perfect, or even the best possible, the view often is that they afford the best solution for our particular conditions and circumstances, even though past history has shown that this is frequently not the case. Many of the fundamental needs of libraries and the purposes of library functions of a particular kind are the same no matter where the library is located, and it can do only disservice to our profession and those whom it exists to aid, if we ignore what is going on in the rest of the world. Those who wish to do so, either because they feel that "our" ways are the best, or for some other reason, should be asked to consider what the development of education, medicine, or archaeology would have been had the teachers, practitioners, and researchers in those fields wholly disregarded achievements produced outside their own countries.

Although librarianship, unlike many other disciplines, has no journal exclusively devoted to comparative studies, two of our periodicals do have avowed and specific international and comparative scope. In an editorial statement in the first issue of the first volume of The Journal of Library History, Philosophy and Comparative Librarianship, the editors write, "It is the aim of the editors of the Journal of Library History to provide in their publication a continuing stream of readable, authoritative material in the subject areas of library history, philosophy, and

comparative librarianship."[28] So far as "comparative librarianship" is concerned, this statement represents a pious, as yet
largely unfulfilled hope. No article in the first volume has anything whatever to do with this subject, and not more than two,
if one adopts a very loose and liberal view, constitute comparative studies in the subsequent volumes.

One of these was published in October 1972 as part of a
"Special Issue on Comparative Librarianship." None of the
rest of the material in this issue is genuinely comparative. The
issue editor writes:

> The JLH Editorial Board began to plan a year ago for an
> issue devoted to comparative librarianship. The result has
> been beset by difficulties of distance, language, cultural dif-
> ferences, and postal systems. . . . We are aware that this
> initial effort falls short of the in-depth comparative analysis
> we had hoped for. We present it, however, with the pride
> due a *fait accompli* and with hopes for future achievement
> to match our present ambitions.[29]

Under the circumstances, it would have been better had the
publication of a "Special Issue on Comparative Librarianship"
been postponed until such time as there was appropriate material to fill it. The same comment may be made about the "Comparative Library Education" issue of the *Journal of Education
for Librarianship*, volume 6 (Spring 1966), which contains not
a single comparative contribution.

The editor of the *International Library Review* writes of the
"need for an independent review devoted to international and
comparative librarianship," and the journal does much better.[30]
While little that has thus far appeared could make much claim
to scholarship, or is concerned with the fundamentals of com-

[28] *The Journal of Library History, Philosophy and Comparative Librarianship*, 1:74 (Jan. 1966).

[29] Ibid., 7:292 (Oct. 1972).

[30] *International Library Review* 1:1 (Jan. 1969).

parative study, the journal has published a number of articles that meet the indispensable criteria of cross-national, cross-societal, or cross-cultural coverage and that make some attempt at explanation.

Note should also be taken, in this connection, of the *UNESCO Bulletin for Libraries* which, since its founding in 1946, has published more international and internationally oriented literature about libraries than any other journal. In so doing, it has rendered an invaluable service in bringing to the attention of the profession information about libraries and librarianship throughout the world, much of which information would almost certainly have remained undisseminated had it not been for UNESCO. Only a very small percentage of the articles appearing in the *Bulletin*, however, may properly be called comparative.

Among other major journals that, now and then, publish articles of a comparative nature are: *College and Research Libraries, Journal of Education for Librarianship, Journal of Librarianship, Library Journal, Library Quarterly, Library Trends, Library World, Libri, Nordisk Tidskrift för Bok og Biblioteksväsen, Wilson Library Bulletin, Zeitschrift für Bibliothekswesen und Bibliographie,* and *Zentralblatt für Bibliothekswesen.*

To the almost wholly negative views expressed and evidence presented thus far in this chapter, there can happily be added a positive note. There are a few solid comparative studies in librarianship that are bright rays in the general darkness, and note should be taken of some of them. What are they and where are they to be found? A partial answer to the second half of the question is that some of them are to be found in rather unlikely places. Three early works may be mentioned first. Even among teachers of comparative librarianship, few appear even to have heard of any of them.

The first of these studies is a work by Maurice Pellisson, *Les Bibliothèques Populaires à l'Étranger et en France* (Paris: Imprimerie Nationale, 1906). Pellisson describes, in successive chapters: the history; controlling legislation and administration; physical plant and organization; role and status of the librarian; and effects (*résultats*) of the public library in the United States, England, Germany, and France. (The author also gives a bird's-eye view of the public library situation in the other European countries, simply to round out the picture; this material is ancillary and in no way essential to the study.)

Following these accounts, there is a concluding chapter in which Pellisson analyzes and synthesizes his findings and provides perceptive explanation for the differences he finds, especially between the public libraries of England and the United States on the one hand, and those of France on the other. Finally, with special reference to the situation in France, the author suggests principles as well as measures which, in his view, underlie the provision of good public library service. Although Pellisson, by his own admission, intended his work as a plea for the improvement of French public libraries, the study is an objective one, solidly based upon fact. It is remarkable that barely a score of publications since Pellisson's so well meet all of the criteria for serious comparative studies in librarianship.

An almost equally early study is Eugène Morel's *Bibliothèques: Essai sur le Développement des Bibliothèques Publiques et de la Librairie dans les Deux Mondes* (2 vols.; Paris: Mercure de France, 1908). Morel at the time was on the staff of the *Bibliothèque Nationale*. His study meets the essential criteria for a good comparative work: it is obviously cross-national; it includes a very large body of carefully selected and analyzed data that, within the constraints of the period at which the study was made and the sources available, are remarkably full; it compares and contrasts these data and provides some synthesis of them; from these syntheses it seeks to arrive at explanations and, at least to some degree, to derive theories and principles. It is a comprehensive study, covering not only the major kinds of libraries in France, Germany, and the United States, but also aspects of librarianship such as administration, cataloging, budget, buildings, and service. The work is far ahead of its time and deserves to be much better known than it is.

A third study that may be considered "early" is Enrique Sparn's *Las Biblotecas con 50,000 y mas Volumenes y su Distribucion Geografica Sobre la Tierra* (Cordoba: National Academy of Sciences, 1924; Miscellaneous Publications, vol. 3, no. 8). At the time he made his study, Sparn was librarian of the Academy. His study is world-wide in scope and shows the distribution, by continents, countries and types of library, of all institutions that he could locate having 50,000 or more volumes. The study is less good than Morel's or Pellisson's in that it provides little in the way either of explanation or principle.

Much more recently, a fellow countryman of Morel's and Pellisson's, Jean Hassenforder, has produced a not dissimilar study, also less well known than it deserves to be. Hassenforder's *Développement Comparé des Bibliothèques Publiques en France, en Grande-Bretagne, et aux États-Unis dans la Seconde Moitié du XIXe Siècle (1850–1914)* (Paris: Cercle de la Librairie, 1967), his dissertation for the degree of doctor of pedagogy, meets all of the criteria for a good comparative work, even though the American university doctoral committee might frown a bit at the somewhat heavy reliance upon secondary sources.

Another little-known study is P. G. J. Overduin's "The Education Librarianship in Some European Countries and in the Transvaal" (*Mousaion* 89–90 [1966]). This 135-page article appears in a journal published in Pretoria. The oddly worded title, which will surely be misleading to many, concerns a study of school libraries and school librarianship in Great Britain, Norway, Sweden, Denmark, the Netherlands, and the Transvaal. After delineating his problem and describing the purpose and method of his inquiry, the author has chapters on each of the six countries. Each of these chapters begins with a general statement, usually including information on population, geography, history, and political, social, and economic factors. Not all of these are given for each country but most are. Following this, there are description and discussion of school library policy and control; the librarian, and his status and education; book stock; library organization and administration; space; and a concluding summary. A final chapter is devoted to comparisons of the situation regarding each of these in the several countries, with considerable explanation of the differences the author found; and to "Recommendations," which is, in part, a statement of principles for satisfactory school library service. In three addenda, Overduin provides the reader with a copy of the questionnaire he submitted to school libraries in the countries; a copy of the questionnaire addressed to the school library administrators; and a list of the fifty-eight schools he visited and thirty-seven individuals with whom he had discussions in the five European countries.

Until the late 1960s, E. I. Šamurin's comparative study of classification systems, *Ocherki po Istorii Bibliotechne-Bibliograficheskoi Klassifikatsii* (2 vols.; Moscow: Vsesoiuznaia Knizhnaia Palata 1955, 1959), was largely inaccessible to Western students. Willi Hoepp's translation, *Geschichte der Bibliothekarisch-Bibliographischen Klassifikation* (2 vols.; Munich: Verlag Dokumentation, 1967, 1968), made the study available at least to those with a good knowledge of German. The title, both in German and Russian, is misleading. This fine study does, to be sure, include historical accounts of all of the major, as well as many minor, little-known classification systems, both library and general, but it is far more than simple history. The work is also a careful analysis of the bases upon which the systems are built, a comparison, in both theoretical and practical terms, of their differences and similarities, explanation of those differences, and the significance of the several schemes. Finally, the study attempts to lay down the fundamentals which should apply to present and future classification schemes.

At least two of Ranganathan's books, one in the field of cataloging and one in the field of classification, are genuinely comparative studies: *Headings and Canons: A Comparative Study of Five Cataloguing Codes,* and *Prolegomena to Library Classification.*[31]

In *Headings and Canons,* Ranganathan analyzes comparatively five major codes as their rules concern choice of headings of various kinds, and does so on the basis of a scientific methodology. This is a comparative analysis, in depth, of the means used by the several codes for determining questions of heading.

Similarly, *Prolegomena* provides a detailed comparative analysis of methods used by seven classification systems in attacking problems in that field. In both works, as in much of the rest of his writing, Ranganathan attempts to construct a general theory or general theories and to propose practicable solutions. However, as Foskett has quite properly pointed out, Ranganathan to some extent vitiates the value of *Prolegomena* in that he subjects his hypotheses only "to the test of incorporation into the Colon Classification" which is in many respects an incomplete scheme.[32]

These are, of course, not the only comparative monographic studies, and there are a few—a very few—journal articles that qualify, but the total number is distressingly small, perhaps no more than twenty or twenty-five altogether.

[31] S. R. Ranganathan, *Headings and Canons: A Comparative Study of Five Cataloguing Codes* (London: Blunt, 1955) and *Prolegomena to Library Classification,* 2nd ed. (London: Library Assn., 1957).

[32] D. J. Foskett, *Science, Humanism, and Libraries* (London: Lockwood, 1964), pp. 180–81.

5

The Dimension of Methodology

There are a number of ways through which man has discovered new knowledge, or "truth," or has supported the validity of what he believes to be true, asserts as truth, or wishes others to believe is true.

Probably as old as man's thought processes is the acquisition of knowledge by deduction, still a legitimate and, at some points, an essential tool in research. Deduction begins with propositions believed or assumed to be true and proceeds logically from these generalizations to arrive at a conclusion which is also true if the original propositions are true. The controlling and operative word here is "if." Unless the original generalizations are supported by demonstrable fact, or happen to be fact without such support, the conclusion will be false. This, obviously, is the great limitation of the method. All libraries acquire reading materials; Branchville is a library; therefore Branchville acquires reading materials; this is deduction in its simplest form, and is true. But in the following proposition, although the logic is just as impeccable, we reject the conclusion because we now know the original proposition, the major premise, to be false: Yellow fever is a contagious disease, transmitted from human to human; John has yellow fever; therefore if we isolate John, others will certainly not contract the disease.

A second means of trying to establish "truth" is through the tenacious and repeated assertion of the proposed fact, without any kind of validating evidence. For example, the provision of qualitatively poor, "trashy," literature in a public library is fully justified because some people can be induced or are able and willing to read only at this level; after they have done so for a while, they will be led to read increasingly better books.

A third means is through the appeal to authority, that is, the citation of the opinions of presumed experts. This means (upon which, because of its nature, the present essay at some points relies more heavily than the writer could wish) also has grave limitations. Who are the experts, how does one select them, how much do they know, how fully do they know, and how should one choose between them, or reconcile their conflicting opinions?[1] Furthermore, unless the views of the experts are the result of careful inquiry and not the mere statement of held beliefs, there is no evidence to support them or way to test their truth or falsity.

Numerous important truths have come about through intuition, "the flash of insight," or serendipity—the law of gravity and the discovery of penicillin, among many others. But these are obviously chancy means which cannot regularly and steadily be relied upon to provide us with explanations over a wide range of relationships in the universe about us.

---

[1] The reader will no doubt have observed the heavy reliance upon this means, particularly in chapters 2 and 3. In the inquiry there on definition, terminology, and purpose, no other primary avenue was available. However, a principal disadvantage of the "reliance upon authority" was not in these cases present, as expert opinion is in virtually unanimous agreement; there was, therefore, no need to choose between conflicting views.

Knowledge also derives directly from man's experience, from the application of trial and error, and often results from the conscious attempt to solve a problem. It is not, on the whole, a very satisfactory method because it is often tied to isolated situations from which—unless the experience is repeated—valid generalizations cannot be drawn, it is seldom systematic and, above all, it cannot readily be applied to the examination or testing of either complicated or abstract relationships.

Finally, there is the method of science, scientific method, which has been found to be, on the whole, the most satisfactory of all methods in all fields, and is the most satisfactory method for comparative studies in librarianship as well.[2]

[2] There are scores, probably hundreds, of works on this subject. The reader's attention is particularly called to the following—titles marked with an asterisk are especially pertinent and helpful to the librarian comparativist: George Z. F. Bereday, *Comparative Method in Education* (New York: Holt, c1964); *Morris R. Cohen and Ernest Nagel, *An Introduction to Logic and Scientific Method* (New York: Harcourt, Brace, 1934); *Maurice Duverger, *An Introduction to the Social Sciences, with Special Reference to Their Methods*, trans. by Malcolm Anderson (London: Allen and Unwin, 1964)—the sections on "Documentary Observation" (categories of documents, statistics, analysis of documents), pp. 75–124; "Direct Extensive Observation" (sampling, questionnaires), pp. 125–77; "Direct Intensive Observation" (interviews, tests of attitudes, participant observation), pp. 178–222; and "Comparative Method," pp. 261–69, are especially useful; *Herbert Goldhor, *An Introduction to Scientific Research in Librarianship* (Washington: U.S. Department of Health, Education and Welfare, 1969; Bureau of Research, Office of Education Final Report, project no. 7-1217), esp. pp. 1–6, 13–23, 40–49, 52, 73, 77–94; *Tyrus Hillway, *Introduction to Research*, 2nd ed. (New York: Houghton Mifflin, 1964); Carlo L. Lastrucci, *The Scientific Approach: Basic Principles of the Scientific Method* (Cambridge, Mass.: Schenkman, 1967); *George J. Mouly, *The Science of Educational Research* (New York: American Book Co., 1963), esp. chapter 4; *Harold J. Noah and Max A. Eckstein, *Toward a Science of Comparative Education* (New York: Macmillan, 1969), esp. chapters 6, 8, 9, 10; F. S. C. Northrop, *The Logic of the Sciences and the Humanities* (New York: Macmillan, 1948); Deobold B. Van Dalen, *Understanding Educational Research: An Introduction*, enl. and rev. ed. (New York: McGraw-Hill, 1966).

But saying it is so does not make it so. The major question to be faced is whether, in fact, we may justifiably speak of and use general scientific method and procedure in connection with serious comparative librarianship inquiry. Herbert Goldhor gives a clear and categorical affirmative answer to the question, so far as librarianship as a whole is concerned, and this answer must inevitably apply also to sub-areas of our discipline, such as comparative librarianship and library history.[3] The affirmative answer applies from logical and practical necessity.

The features of this procedure which commend themselves to us and which must be of concern to us are, first, that it is concerned with facts, and not with belief, or unsupported opinion; second, that it brings empirical evidence to bear upon hypotheses and other statements advanced; third, that it strives at every point for objectivity; fourth, that it aims at precise description by analysis of the data concerning properties and relationships of observed phenomena; and, finally, that it seeks explanation through the formulation of general statements. These considerations are elaborated upon hereafter.

Harold J. Noah and Max Eckstein trace the development of comparative education through a number of stages beginning with "Travellers' Tales," "Educational Borrowing," and "International Cooperation," to, finally, "Social Science Explanation."[4] Comparative librarianship exhibits the same stages except that, as considered in the preceding chapter, we are only just beginning to approach, here and there, the final stage.

In the following discussion of scientific method, there is no thought that the humanistic and philosophical traditions of librarianship should be abandoned or ignored. Many problems will be studied and contributions made for which quantifiable data may not be the only, or even the chief base. Numerous bibliographical studies are of this kind.

3 Goldhor, *Introduction to Scientific Research*, esp. pp. 13–37.

4 Noah and Eckstein, *Comparative Education*, pp. 1–79.

In addition, many problems we should like to study, that is, hypotheses we should like to test, cannot be undertaken through the means stated above and discussed in this chapter, simply because the data are not available and cannot be acquired. One such, for illustration, is the following: an increase in the number of doctoral programs in comparative librarianship would substantially increase the quantity and quality of research in comparative librarianship. As we have, world-wide, produced only half a dozen doctorates in comparative librarianship, and as these have not yet published anything beyond their dissertations, there is no data base for testing the hypothesis. The best that could be done in this case would be to study a comparable field, like education, and see whether, as doctoral programs in comparative education have increased (as they have), the quantity and quality of research in comparative education have also increased. It would then be necessary to argue, by analogy, that the same result would occur in librarianship. Such an argument, however persuasive, falls very considerably short of certainty.

Further, as discussed in chapter 2, questions involving moral and value judgments also fall beyond the confines—and the ability—of "social science explanation." The opinions of "experts" may be gathered—and counted—to rate the quality of the poetry of Robert Frost, Emily Dickinson, and Edwin Arlington Robinson, to be sure, but the ultimate question, how "good" is the poetry, involves an esthetic judgment. Many other questions, some of them of considerable importance, are exceedingly difficult to test precisely, or they resist precise testing entirely, as, for instance: In the long run, it would be better for libraries to use unexpected budgetary allotments to employ librarians for a year than to buy and process additional volumes.

Nevertheless, most studies of the library as a social institution will have to use the scientific method and the techniques developed for the social sciences. The basic methods of scientific inquiry cannot be ignored even in such an investigation as the comparison of book selection policy.

Comparative librarianship, like comparative anthropology, comparative law, comparative philology (now often simply called linguistics), comparative government, comparative sociology, and comparative education, is not a separate science or discipline. It is, rather, a part of a discipline, a field, characterized by its *primary* method (comparison), its scope (cross-societal, cross-cultural), its inter-disciplinary nature, and its aim (the search for similarities and differences and the attempt to explain the latter). Comparative librarianship is related to and coordinated with the discipline as a whole in much the same way as its closely related sister, library history. What library history strives to discern in studying and explaining the vertical, or past, development of libraries, comparative librarianship generally attempts to achieve through a horizontal examination, that is, a view of the patterns and differentiations of present library structures. In some sense, at least, comparative librarianship is a prolongation into the present of library history.

Comparative librarianship differs from other sub-areas of librarianship, such as the sociology of libraries or the history of libraries, in that it has no direct relationship to another *single* discipline (sociology, history).

It is going much too far, however, to say that comparative librarianship, or comparative anything else, is *only* a method and an indication of the primary scope and approach. Its data are sometimes unique to itself, that is, cannot be secured through other methods, and almost none of its findings can be duplicated through other means. There is, in other words, a *content* of comparative librarianship, just as there is a content of library history—or a content of comparative education, or of comparative anthropology.

The methodological steps of serious comparative study in librarianship are fundamentally no different from those in any other social science inquiry. The essential, the indispensable beginning point of such inquiry, indeed, of almost all serious inquiry, is the hypothesis. It is so central to sound investigation,

116

and its advantages are so great that Goldhor, for instance, in his excellent study devotes more than a seventh of his entire text proper to its discussion.[5]

Synthesizing the definitions in the standard English-language dictionaries, an hypothesis may be described as a statement which asserts a presumed relationship between facts or variables. It is a *tentative* conjecture which provisionally assigns a cause to known facts and serves as a basis for their arrangement and classification. It is also a starting point for investigation—these facts are studied and new, pertinent data are collected—which leads to the proof or disproof of the conjecture. An hypothesis is a guess—an intelligent and enlightened guess, often a highly informed guess, but a guess nonetheless—as to the relationship between two, or sometimes more, variables or sets of facts.

An hypothesis usually has its origin in a question of the nature, "Is it true that . . . (if so, why)?" or "Why is it that . . . ?"[6]

[5] Goldhor, *Introduction to Scientific Research*, pp. 52–73, 174–79. A very large number of other works treat the topic extensively. Perhaps most useful of these for the student of comparative librarianship is Noah and Eckstein, *Comparative Education*, esp. pp. 92–99, 125–28, 131–34, 176–80, and 186–87. The reader who wishes a more detailed treatment than is given in the present study is urged to consult these two works.

[6] The treatises that deal with this topic insist that proper hypotheses, or at least the best ones, are not generated from empirical observations of variables, but are derived rather from (a broader) theory, or, as some put it, from laws, scientific principles, or paradigms. The grounds for this view are chiefly two: first, that without a theoretical basis, an hypothesis is likely to be insubstantial and result in the more or less obvious; and, second, that whereas most hypotheses deal typically with only one relationship, a theory encompasses many and offers the potential for understanding a large number of kinds of phenomena.

The still largely pragmatic nature of librarianship and its embryonic state as a "science" are best evidenced by the paucity of theory in the field in general and in comparative librarianship most particularly. For the immediate future, therefore, we cannot expect to be able to generate many hypotheses from theory. However, in the social sciences, and even in the scientifically mature physical sciences, hypotheses can be and often are

One reads, for instance, in the current reports of a few university libraries that undergraduate student use of library books increased significantly following the provision by the universities of separate library facilities for undergraduates. These statements might naturally evoke the twofold question, "Is this *really* true and, if so, is it *generally* true?" The "really" asks whether the increased book use is, as implied, in fact directly attributable to the establishment of undergraduate library facilities, and not the result of other, unnamed factors. The "generally" asks (if the answer to the first part of the question is affirmative) whether the relationship—provision of undergraduate library facilities/increased library book use—holds for other institutions as well as the ones that reported. The twofold question can then be stated in the form of an hypothesis that encompasses both its parts: the provision by universities of separate library facilities for undergraduates will significantly increase the library book use of undergraduate students. A study to test this hypothesis could be undertaken for the United States alone, in which case the study would clearly not be a comparative one, and the proposition, if proved, would not necessarily hold elsewhere. Or the study could be carried out in institutions of Great Britain and the United States, in which case the study would be a comparative one, and the proposition, if proved, would make possible a wider generalization. In either case, however, as in the testing of all hypotheses, it would be necessary to eliminate, or hold constant, the potential effects of *other* variables upon the one being studied. In the present instance, that is, we should need to eliminate, or hold constant, the possible influence upon the amount of undergraduate library book use of changes in instructional methods; increases in book purchases; size of book collections; changes in the nature of the student population; in short, all possible influences which, regardless of the provision of sepa-

---

developed quite independently of a broader theory, and for the most part we shall have to be content to do so for some time.

118

rate facilities, might have caused increases in the library book use of undergraduates.

The overriding importance of the hypothesis is that it serves the investigator as a guide to the kind, sources, and number of data he should acquire. Without a guiding hypothesis there is no way of knowing what facts, or what sorts of facts from what countries or kinds of libraries, are to be sought, nor even when enough of them have been gathered. Without an hypothesis, useless data may be collected, or data from the wrong places, or too few data, or unnecessarily large amounts of data.

Reading of the literature of comparative and international librarianship suggests that the authors of much of it began with no clearly defined hypothesis. The result is that many publications consist of little more than the indiscriminate and undigested amassing of library and other data, and are characterized by the primacy of a priori assumptions over both the fact-collecting process and the conclusions, if any, derived from the facts.

Another major fact of the hypothesis is that it serves as a measure for evaluating the data which have been collected and presented—evaluation by the investigator himself and by subsequent readers.

Ideally, an hypothesis should express a relationship which is universal, invariable, and causal. In the above hypothesis, if repeated studies, undertaken wherever universities have provided separate facilities for undergraduates, should consistently show that such provision always significantly increased their library book use, we should be able to make a universally applicable generalization.

Similarly, the hypothesis as stated also places no limit on time. It implies that the relationship is not only true now, but has been true in the past and will always be true in the future. If the hypothesis were repeatedly tested today and found to conform with the facts, but testing ten years hence produced contrary results, it could not be considered invariable and would have to be revised to indicate its time limitation and, more important, the nature of the difference(s) which produced the altered results.

The hypothesis as stated says nothing, however, about the possible reason or cause of the relationship, if proved true. The causal element is important not simply because the statement of "why" best leads us to an understanding of the phenomena about us, but also because it forces upon the investigator a thorough and deeper understanding of the phenomena he is studying. While it is of some interest and may be of some use to know the fact, if it is a fact, that undergraduate use of library books will increase when a university provides separate library facilities for undergraduates, this fact bears real significance solely as it becomes part of a system of cause and effect.

So, to the stated hypothesis, one might, for example, add: library book use of undergraduate students will increase because their books are all brought together in one place (the undergraduate library) and are made readily and fully accessible to them. The proposition is now clearly much more difficult to test; we should have to provide additional and more complex controls. But if the proposition, upon investigation, were found to be true, it might lead us to a further and more significant hypothesis, namely, that ready accessibility to the books they need is the major factor influencing the amount of undergraduate students' library book use.

It might be discovered, however, that though complete accessibility was the cause of the increased use in institutions (or countries) where significant increase was found, such increase was not at all present in some other institutions (or countries), and there accessibility had no effect upon use. This limitation of the universality of the hypothesis might then lead us to hypothesize further that the proposition holds true only where instructional methods are such as to require student use of library materials; in those parts of the world where the student can be assured of satisfactory performance solely by memorizing a text and what the teacher tells him in class, the proposition will not be true, and no matter how accessible library materials are made, students will not be persuaded to use them because they have no need to do so.

It is also conceivable, of course, that we might find that, though the use of library books by undergraduates significantly increased, the accessibility of the books was not, or was not the principal, cause of the increase; in such case, a different causal element would have to be introduced and tested, such as increased faculty interest in the role of the library in undergraduate education.

Although an hypothesis should, ideally, express a relationship which is universal and invariable, the fact is, that in the social sciences, innumerable hypotheses can usefully be tested which are neither the one nor the other. In librarianship, in particular, one may go further than this. The paucity of our research on almost all aspects of the field suggests that we need many studies, the hypotheses of which are restricted either in time or space, or both. If the space restriction is such that the study is not cross-societal, it is obviously not a comparative one. This is not grounds for arguing that it should not be undertaken, especially if the time, means, or competence of the investigator prevents a larger-scale effort. Learning about the effects of important variables, even in a limited setting, is clearly valuable to us, and research of a non-comparative nature may lead to intermediate-level theory. Other investigators, then, may undertake similar studies in other spatial contexts, and all of these investigations, taken together, may lead to a comparative result and the testing or proof of a more nearly universal hypothesis. In the discussion of area studies (pages 42–43) it was suggested that we need far more of them than we have, and that their production will facilitate the work of the comparative investigator. Similarly, we need more studies which test hypotheses of restricted kinds. It is probably true, in view of the time-consuming nature of solid comparative studies, that we shall produce few of them until

121

there are many more good area studies and good studies testing restricted hypotheses. Those who produce such studies will receive our gratitude and praise, even though the studies themselves are in no sense comparative.

The subsequent steps, after establishment of the hypothesis, consist of:

1. The systematic collection and the accurate description of data bearing upon the problem or situation
2. Interpretation, that is, the analysis of these data in terms of their social relationships and by accepted techniques
3. Juxtaposition, that is, the examination of the data bearing upon the problem, or situation, in the one society or country with those in the other to establish the framework in which they may be compared
4. The comparison, or comparisons, themselves, of the problem or situation
5. The attempt to arrive at causes, explanations, and principles.[7]

There is, in a sense, a still further step, namely, the testing for validity and reliability of the conclusions of step 5 through other studies of the same situation or problem in other cross-national or cross-societal contexts. But the enormously complicated and time-consuming nature of the study of even a rela-

[7] The sophisticated and knowledgeable reader may feel that this statement offers a rather one-sided, restricted, too simple view and, strictly speaking, it does. Axiomatic-deductive model building, abstract theorizing or reasoning, independent of empirical observations and checks, the abstract calculus, and mathematical models play increasingly important roles in much scientific investigation today. However, in the social sciences generally, and in librarianship in particular, the level of development as a "science," the state of our knowledge, and of our available data are such that we are likely to have to be content for some time to come with non-mathematical, non-paradigmatic methods. If this be granted, the basic method, briefly outlined in the section to which this footnote refers, is the one we shall have to use. We need not feel like second-class citizens because of it; most scientific investigation, not only in the social sciences but also in the physical sciences, still travels this same basic path.

tively small problem or aspect of librarianship will normally prevent the individual investigator from doing very much of this. Comparative librarianship, as a total effort, however, must take this final step except in those few cases where the study can include the whole universe of relevant phenomena.

The enormous advantages of the scientific method, fully demonstrated hundreds of thousands of times in virtually every field of human inquiry, may be simply and briefly summarized. It is dianoetic and factually based—it does not depend on chance, insight, intuition, inspiration, or the happenstance event; it may be used by anyone who has mastered its procedures to investigate almost every kind of phenomenon, problem, and relationship; it is largely self-correcting, in that the data and techniques used may be re-examined and are open to public scrutiny; it minimizes the possibility, inherent in all inquiry, of bias on the part of the investigator, a possibility to which studies in librarianship are peculiarly susceptible; it is consistent and widely understood; and its results provide stepping stones that lead to further inquiry, either of a verifying or refined nature or along new paths, and building blocks upon which further extension of our knowledge may be based.

Librarianship has advanced a considerable distance since the days when a very large percentage of the profession viewed with distrust the use of quantitative measures, beyond the simplest counting of loan statistics, acquisitions, book stock, personnel, and monetary and spatial units, in the treatment of library phenomena. The distrust, fear, and even animosity with which the social science-based and scientifically oriented Graduate Library School of the University of Chicago was met less than half a century ago, are a matter of historical record. In recent years, the founding of schools, not only in the United States but also in Great Britain and on the Continent, much further removed from earlier humanistic traditions of librarianship raises neither question nor outcry today. The contrast, too, between the professional literature thirty or forty years ago and that being published today, even in relatively "popular" journals, is also very striking. Nonetheless, a few words about quantification in the context of the discussion in this chapter may not be out of order.

The assumption is not unknown in librarianship even today that quantification is simply a question of "nose-counting," that it is or should be severely limited to physical objects that are obviously and readily countable—number of books, loans, seats, units of space, and so on—and that almost everything else must or should be handled by non-quantitative means. Although some kinds of information are not readily amenable to quantification and others (such as the intensity of one's appreciation of *Hamlet*) are impossible to measure precisely, the limits of the application of quantification are far broader than generally believed. The hard fact is, indeed, that the quantitative approach, at least in some degree, is forced upon us for most of what we wish to study.

Consider, for illustration, the public libraries of two countries and the question of patrons' access to library materials. The results of even the simplest, most unsophisticated investigation, showing that in certain libraries the patrons have free access and in others they do not, produce a yes/no table or listing (binary scale), and the yes-no items not only can be counted, but would inevitably have to be counted in order to make statements about the two groups of libraries. Few would be willing to let the matter rest here, if only because the data thus far shown raise more questions than they answer. We note in the responses from the "yes" group, for instance, the recurring statement that "all patrons have free, ready access to all library materials." Examination of the actual situation, however, reveals the fact that patrons do not have ready and free access in some, most, or all of the libraries to archival materials, manuscripts, rare books, erotica, anti-government publications, and much-in-demand, easily lost reference works. Consequently, the "yes" scale or listing must be refined in a way to show the extent, amount, or degree of "free and ready access," and the results of this refinement must, again, be counted if they are to be meaningfully used. The libraries could then be arranged in order (an ordinal scale) to show the extent or frequency of ready access to different kinds of library materials. A still further refinement would produce a cardinal scale, indicating how much access existed.

The point of the foregoing is to suggest that little of what we wish to investigate concerning libraries is not amenable to at least some quantification, that quantification in most investigation cannot be avoided, and that, in fact, we should not attempt to avoid it. On the contrary, according to Maurice Duverger:

> The expression of phenomena by figures and symbols allows a large number to be compared simultaneously, their respective characteristics can be set against one another with great accuracy, and their analysis taken much further. In striving to introduce "quantification" and mathematics into their disciplines as far as possible, specialists in the social sciences, contrary to what many laymen think, are not merely deferring to a fashion, but are recognizing that mathematics provides analytical tools incomparably more effective than classical comparative methods.[8]

The problem of methodology in comparative librarianship, then, is not one of inventing new methods of dealing with data —though we may be fortunate enough to achieve some of this sometime—but rather of adopting and adapting ideas, methods, and techniques that have already proved their worth in other fields *which deal with the same general kinds of data.* As already noted, descriptions of these methods may be found in scores of texts in sociology, education, and political science. Thus, theoretically at least, it should be possible to construct a general theory of the Western free public library involving consideration of the relations between that institution and the maintenance of a healthy, democratic society. Such a theory should be built inductively, but the objective should be to present it—in so far

[8] Duverger, *Introduction to the Social Sciences*, p. 277.

as possible—deductively, that is, in terms of principles from which the limits and potentialities of the library under particular conditions could be deduced. Is such a library, in fact, essential to the maintenance of a democratic society? In what ways and to what extent is it necessary? In what degree or to what extent must its characteristics—governance, locations, incidence, book stock, personnel, budget, access—be present if it is to fulfill this function?

Obviously such a theory could not be developed without extraordinarily careful and intensive investigation, and it could hardly be done in a meaningful way, except comparatively. The informed reader does not have to be reminded that the foregoing is only one of scores (more likely hundreds) of major fields of inquiry the profession might, but has not, undertaken.

Comparison is a fundamental and essential part of all inquiry and investigation. Comparison is involved, either directly or indirectly, in *all methods* of investigation: inductive, deductive, historical, empirical, statistical, scientific, quantitative, *a priori*, *a posteriori*, experimental, and all of the other words and terms used to describe such methods. Nearly forty years ago, John Dewey wrote in his work on logic:

> Comparison . . . is a name for *all* operations in which identities and incompatibilities in evidential force are determined. It is a name for any and all of the operations by means of which alleged or provisional data are determined to *be* data with respect to the problem set by a given indeterminate situation; by which some facts are determined to be the "facts of the case" in hand and other facts not to be. . . . It is a blanket term for the entire complex of operations by which some existences are selectively instituted as data and other existential materials are eliminated as having nothing to do with the case. . . .[9]

[9] John Dewey, *Logic: The Theory of Inquiry* (New York: Holt, c1938), p. 184.

As Harald Høffding expressed the concept, "It has been said that 'to think is to compare—to find difference and similarity.' "[10] In short, comparison is everywhere implicit in serious inquiry, and exists before it becomes explicit in comparative method.

Evidence of the significance early attached to the comparative method, which itself is grounded in general scientific method, may be gained from Edward A. Freeman's evaluation: "The establishment of the Comparative Method of study has been the greatest intellectual achievement of our time."[11] Later he writes:

> I do not for a moment hesitate to say that the discovery of the Comparative Method in philology, in mythology— let me add in politics and history and the whole range of human thought—marks a stage in the progress of the human mind at least as great and memorable as the revival of Greek and Latin learning. The great contribution of the nineteenth century to the advance of human knowledge may boldly take its stand alongside of the great contribution of the fifteenth.[12]

Indeed in some fields the comparative is so central to serious inquiry, and deemed so pervasive, that the word itself is often down-graded, or omitted entirely. Thus, as long ago as the end of the last century, Durkheim, the distinguished pioneer of the universities of Bordeaux and Paris who exerted such a profound

[10] Quoted by Frede Castberg, *Freedom of Speech in the West* (Oslo: Oslo Univ. Pr., 1960), p. 4 from Harald Høffding, *Kort Oversigt over den Nyere Filosofis Historie*, 4th ed. (Copenhagen, 1910), p. 1. Castberg's fine study is a comparative investigation of public law as it pertains to freedom of speech in France, the United States, and Germany. The study pays due attention to the historical development of political freedom of speech, points up and explains the differences in judicial and political control in the three countries, and draws a number of general conclusions.

[11] Edward A. Freeman, *Comparative Politics* (London: MacMillan, 1873), p. 1.

[12] Ibid., pp. 301–2.

influence upon at least two generations of comparativists in social studies, maintained: "Comparative sociology is not a particular branch of sociology; it is sociology itself, in so far as it ceases
to be purely descriptive and aspires to account for facts."[13]

Similarly, of another field A. Eustace Haydon wrote, "the term
comparative religion has always been awkward and unsatisfac-
tory. It may be regarded as synonymous with the science of
religion. . . ."[14]

Comparison implies membership of the things compared
within the same or a very similar class, namely, that there is a
sharing of at least one significant quality *in sufficient degree* to
warrant meaningful comparison. For this reason, we cannot usefully compare oranges and tennis balls (even though they both
share the quality of "roundness"), but we can compare tennis
balls and other kinds of balls; we cannot usefully compare children's and university library book collections, but we can compare at least some aspects of national and university libraries.
Although the book collections of children's and university libraries share the "significant quality" of books, the nature of the two
collections (including the purpose for which they are developed
and maintained) is so vastly different that the quality is not
shared in "sufficient degree" to warrant meaningful comparison.

A further aspect of "sufficient degree" needs to be noted,
namely complexity. Comparison of the office of chief librarian of
cities of over a million population in the world would be possible and meaningful. But comparison of this office with the position of village librarian, though possible, would not be a mean-

---

[13] Émile Durkheim, *The Rules of Sociological Method*, trans. Sarah A.
Solovay and John H. Mueller, ed. George E. G. Catlin (Glencoe, Ill.,
Free Pr., 1950), p. 139. The original French reads: "La sociologie comparée n'est pas une branche particulière de la sociologie; c'est la sociologie
même, en tant qu'elle cesse d'être purement descriptive et aspire à rendre
compte des faits." *Les Règles de la Méthode Sociologique* (Paris: Germer
Baillière, 1895), p. 169.

[14] A. Eustace Haydon, "Comparative Religion," *Encyclopedia of the
Social Sciences* 4:131.

ingful enterprise and could have only very superficial results, because the complexity of the positions is too different. Similarly, the administrative procedures of the Library of Congress cannot validly and usefully be compared with those of the national libraries of Cyprus or Ethiopia.

These elements (besides the cross-societal) are essential to satisfactory comparative study:

1. The phenomena being investigated must have a fundamental similarity—they may not be wholly different.
2. The phenomena may not be completely identical.
3. There must be absolute clarity concerning which particular characteristics (that is, aspects of libraries) are being considered, and this requires careful delimitation and definition.
4. There must be description and analysis of the similarities and differences among the various elements being compared.
5. There must be explanation of the differences.

Our principal concerns are with institutions—that is, libraries as physical entities—and with their functions. The latter, in turn, divides itself into what may be called internal functions and activities, such as administration and the technical processes, and external and sociological functions having to do with service. At all points, further, we are concerned with the influences of the entire relevant social milieu upon the phenomena observed.

The difficulties and dangers in the comparison of phenomena of a social nature are readily apparent when we ask such questions as the following: Is the public library in Czechoslovakia or Hungary really the same thing as the public library in Sweden? Does the administrative responsibility of the university librarian mean the same thing in Japan as it does in Germany, Great Britain, or the United States? Is the concept "qualified beginning professional" the same in Austria, Italy, and Yugoslavia as it is in Israel? The fact that negative answers must be given to a precise interpretation of all of these questions does not mean that the juxtaposed situations may not be compared. It points, rather, to the necessity of defining precisely what is being compared, making crystal clear the nature of the differences of the phenomena being compared, and describing the probable effects of those differences.

It is of cardinal importance, accordingly, that we guard against the ever-present danger of making artificial comparisons that are based either on distortions or inaccurate understanding of the phenomena compared. In general, this danger increases directly with increase in distance and context; the danger, that is, is greater in comparing an American and a Japanese situation than in comparing an American and a Canadian one.

The use of the comparative method in the social disciplines, therefore, involves a fundamental assumption that needs to be further considered. It is whether phenomena observed in one society—phenomena influenced by the traditions, the social conditions, the customs and attitudes of people, and so on—can actually be compared with those of others. As every society is the unique product of its own particular history and traditions, the question that arises is if one society may be truly compared with any other, as a practice or situation in one society that may appear the same as its counterpart in another may not really be the same.

While it is true, of course, that every society and every individual in it is unique, it does not therefore follow that comparison is impossible. All scientific investigation rests upon the assumption that characteristics of the universe, or part-universe, can, in fact, be determined and compared. Thus, although it is quite true that no two individuals are absolutely identical, it is also true that all normal persons have two arms, legs, ears, and eyes, and a single nose, chin, and forehead, as well as many other characteristics.

There have, of course, been dissenters to the view that comparison in the social sciences is valid, or even possible. Such dissent is now seldom heard, presumably because of the very large number of excellent studies which have demonstrated the affirmative. Very few responsible writers today would support Malinowski's opinion of thirty years ago, that "the comparative method is wrong, comparing incomparables," because "every cultural institution must be understood as a unique product of the cultural whole in which it developed."[15]

It is obvious that, although comparison is fundamental in all study and is involved in every type and kind of inquiry, and although the comparative method is simply an application of fundamental scientific method, there can be no such thing as a single technique of comparison, applicable alike, let us say, to anthropology, anatomy, law, religion, linguistics, and librarianship. The reason, obviously, is that the data with which these disciplines are concerned differ greatly from each other and therefore require different methods of handling. The difference is especially notable as between the physical and biological sciences on the one hand, and the social sciences on the other, and the two poles of difference are between mathematics and the physical sciences at one end, and the social sciences at the other. The data of the physical sciences are almost wholly, and those of the biological sciences largely, precisely quantifiable and controllable. To be sure, some of the data of the social sciences, amounts of money spent for a certain purpose, for instance, are also precisely quantifiable and statistically controllable. However, the single most important element—the human being—in almost all social inquiry cannot readily be controlled, and can be experimented with in limited ways only. His motivations, purposes, likes and dislikes, and reactions to different kinds of social situations are difficult, if not impossible, both to measure precisely and to control.

Because of the inherent differences in the kinds of data dealt with, the generalizations and principles capable of being drawn

15 E. R. Service, "Cultural Evolution," *International Encyclopedia of the Social Sciences* 5:227.

from studies in social fields, including librarianship, cannot be expected to be of the same immutability, precision, and ultimate provability as are usually implied and understood when we speak of a "law of physics." Such laws are based upon the quantitative measurement and the determinable reactions of inanimate objects.

The determination of causation in a social science like ours is infinitely more difficult and, for that reason, likely to be less unarguably provable, precisely because our phenomena, unlike those of the physical sciences, cannot be isolated from their contexts. One may place gas in a container, apply heat and pressure, and discover that the gas expands in direct proportion to increase in temperature, and inversely to increase in pressure. We cannot, in anything like the same way, "apply" an increase in administrative authority to middle-management library positions and determine the results of that increase. A whole range of other factors—variables—including the leadership qualities of the administrators, their relations with their subordinates, the nature of the latter, and any number of possible differences in the "before" and "after" situation make precise measurement of the facts of the change difficult—even if we could, with a stroke of the pen, increase the administrative authority of a given number of middle managers.

The comparative method, by gathering as many facts from as wide an area as possible, serves as a substitute for the direct, controllable experiment.

Consequently, all of the social sciences are bound to accept that they are not, and cannot be, "scientific" in precisely the same way and to the same degree as are the physical and biological sciences. Inevitably, therefore, we must, for the foreseeable future, be satisfied with the results, that is, with explanations, generalizations, and principles which are often only approximations, or applicable within rather narrow and well-defined limits only.

This does not mean, however, that generalization in the social disciplines is impossible, that such generalizations are the results of little more than guesswork, or that they are without real significance.

We should not permit ourselves, therefore, particularly in considering the validity of findings in social studies, including librarianship, the hypnotic preoccupation of comparison with the exact sciences that held education for so long. In point of fact, the natural sciences are not equally exact—witness, for example the difference between biology and geology—and even physics and chemistry today find themselves involved with non-measurable quantities and approximations.

Many physicists, in fact, at present acknowledge that physical laws are essentially laws of probability of a statistical nature. Consequently, although scientific explanation, scientific law, and the scientific method which produces them can and should mean with us what they mean in other disciplines, the difference between determinism in the physical sciences and a social science like ours is a difference of degree and of achievable exactitude, rather than a difference of kind.

In point of fact, it is not at all difficult to advance supportable universal generalizations about social phenomena in most fields, including librarianship. The difficulty with most such generalizations is that they may readily be criticized as being either obvious or unimportant. For example, there does not appear to be any exception to the generalization that all libraries acquire their materials either through purchase, gift, exchange, the provisions of copyright or other laws (such as P.L. 480 in the United States, a kind of gift), or a combination of two or more of these. The generalization is, in the first place so obvious, so much a matter of simple common sense, as to be considered trivial. Further, the generalization tells us nothing about the important matters within it, such as what kinds of libraries in what countries secure which kinds and amounts of their books from each of these sources, and with what effects upon the libraries' collections and services. We can only hope that attention to serious comparative study will, in time, produce supportable generalizations which, though they may not be so sweeping as the one just suggested, will be more substantive. However, as R. B. Schlesinger has said for the law, we shall have to acquire a large volume of data regarding specific library matters and solutions of problems common to different kinds of libraries, in different places, before significant generalizations will be possible. Consequently, we cannot expect soon to see the formulation of meaningful, widely applicable general principles.[16]

Richard B. Braithwaite has suggested, along this line, a distinction between sciences at different stages of development:

> If [a] science is in a highly developed stage, as in physics, the laws which have been established will form a hierarchy in which many special laws appear as logical consequences of a small number of highly general laws expressed in a very sophisticated manner; if the science is in an early stage of development—what is sometimes called its "natural-history" stage—the laws may be merely the generalizations involved in classifying things into various classes.[17]

From this point of view, librarianship is not in a highly developed stage, and even less highly developed is comparative librarianship. Nevertheless, causal explanation is both possible and necessary for us, just as it is for other not highly developed disciplines like sociology and political science.[18]

Even comparative sociology has not yet produced anything

[16] R. B. Schlesinger, "The Nature of General Principles of Law," *General Report* (Hamburg: International Academy of Comparative Law, 1962), p. 23.

[17] Richard B. Braithwaite, *Scientific Explanation; A Study of the Function of Theory, Probability and Law in Science* (New York: Harper, 1960), p. 1.

[18] Cf., e.g., Max Weber, *The Methodology of the Social Sciences* (Glencoe, Ill.: Free Pr., 1949); Émile Durkheim, *Rules*, p. 95; and A. R. Radcliffe-Brown, *A Natural Science of Society* (Glencoe, Ill.: Free Pr., c1957), esp. pp. 69 ff.

which resembles a natural "law" in the physical science sense. But sociology has demonstrated that the rigorous application of the fundamental methods of scientific inquiry in comparative studies can produce valid and verifiable explanations of important social phenomena. Examples are Émile Durkheim's study which established the social causes of suicide, and Max Weber's classic work.[19]

Although, in a fundamental sense, the methodology of comparative librarianship is the same as that of any social discipline —indeed, in the most fundamental sense, the same as that of most scientific inquiry—in a much broader sense, the techniques of comparative librarianship will in part be determined by the nature of the study. That is, if an investigator wishes to examine the relationship between the sources and amounts of financial support of medium-sized public libraries, however defined, in the Netherlands and Norway, and the nature and effectiveness of library service, much of his technique will be drawn from, and his data will be concerned with economics, government, and sociology. Clearly, also, he will need a substantial knowledge of statistics, as well as a familiarity with at least those parts of the history of the two countries which have influenced the phenomena he is observing.

Accordingly, the study of comparative librarianship and comparative librarianship studies are, without exception, interdisciplinary. Even such a narrowly professional investigation as that of differing national or regional cataloging codes or classification systems could not be prosecuted satisfactorily without attention to semantics, logic, etymology, and the history and nature of classification generally. Comparative librarianship, consequently, as a field of scholarly investigation (and even in teaching) draws

19 Émile Durkheim, *Suicide: A Study in Sociology*, trans. John A. Spalding and George Simpson (London: Routledge and Paul, 1952); Max Weber, *Max Weber on Law in Economy and Society*, ed. Max Rheinstein, trans. Edward Shils and Max Rheinstein (Cambridge: Harvard University Pr., 1954).

upon and requires consideration of the ancillary disciplines as much as librarianship itself.

Of all the social sciences, the one most important for the comparativist is history. It is most important because it is the only one which can never be dispensed with entirely. This is so for a special reason that suggests the desirability of a brief discussion of the relationship between history and comparative study in the other social sciences.

Émile Durkheim stated the case with great clarity and force as early in his writing as *The Rules of Sociological Method*. He contended that, although the causes of social phenomena can be determined only through presently operative variables, such variables can be really understood only with a knowledge of the history which produced the present social milieu.

Later, in another place, he defends this position with these words:

> It is perhaps true that busy sociologists will find this procedure unnecessarily complicated. In order to understand social phenomena of the day in sufficient degree . . . is it not enough to observe them as they are given in our actual experience and is it not a work of vain erudition to undertake research into their most distant origins?—But this quick method is full of illusions. One does not know social reality if one views it from the outside only and if one ignores its sub-structure. In order to know how it is, it is necessary to know how it has come to be, that is to say to have followed in history the manner in which it has been progressively formed. . . . It is indispensable to have studied the social forms of the past. . . . To understand the present it is necessary to go outside of it.[20]

[20] *L'Année Sociologique* 2:v (1899), my translation. The original French text reads as follows: "Peut-être, il est vrai, les sociologues pressés trouveront-ils cette procédure inutilement compliquée. Pour comprendre les phénomènes sociaux l'aujourd'hui dans la mesure nécessaire pour en diriger l'évolution, ne suffit-il pas de les observer tels qu'ils sont donnés dans notre expérience actuelle et n'est-ce pas faire une oeuvre de vaine érudition que de se met-

The comparativist, in testing his hypothesis, gathers data concerning the problem he is studying, organizes and analyzes them, and examines them in the light of relevant sociological, political, economic, educational, and other factors of the social milieu in which the data exist. But all of these factors exist as they are as the result of historical development, and they can be fully understood only through a knowledge of that development, that is, through a knowledge of history. If the historian has not already provided that history—which is sometimes the case with respect to developing countries, for example—the comparativist will be obliged to use the techniques of historical research to provide it for himself. "The historian" may be the educational, political, library, social, or cultural historian. The cardinal point is that almost nothing can be satisfactorily studied solely on the basis of the facts existing at present, but must be examined in the light of the forces that produced them, in the light, that is, of history.

This basic view has been held by, and is exemplified in, the writings of virtually every comparativist of standing in the social sciences since Durkheim's day. Limiting the topic to the field of education, one may mention the work of C. Arnold Anderson, William W. Brickman, Abraham Flexner, Nicholas Hans, Franz Hilker, Isaac L. Kandel, Paul Monroe, Sir Michael Sadler, Peter Sandiford, Friedrich Schneider, and Charles H. Thurber, simply as examples.[21]

---

tre à la recherche de leurs origines les plus éloignées?—Mais cette méthode rapide est grosse d'illusions. On ne connait pas la réalité sociale si on ne l'a vue que du dehors et si l'on en ignore la substructure. Pour savoir comment elle est faite, il faut savoir comment elle s'est faite, c'est-à-dire avoir suivi dans l'histoire la manière dont elle s'est progressivement composée. Pour pouvoir, avec quelques chances de succès, dire ce que sera, ce que doit être la société de demain, il est indispensable d'avoir étudié les formes sociales du passé le plus lointain. Pour comprendre le présent, il faut en sortir."

[21] C. Arnold Anderson, "Methodology of Comparative Education," *International Review of Education* 7 (1961); William W. Brickman, "Com-

This discussion may be made specific by considering the universities, and their libraries, of England, Germany, and the United States. In England, which for more than half a millennium had only two universities, there was, at least until fairly recently, a strictly elitist attitude toward higher education. There was also, among many other things, a special view of liberal education and of its role in the development of personality and moral character. What was studied was less important than the gains to be derived from concentrated application, close contact with wise and learned teachers, and with the great minds of literature—and even from chapel and the playing field.

Germany also had an elitist view of higher education but, in contrast to England, it had created more than a score of permanent universities by the early part of the nineteenth century. What was studied mattered very much, and the university was not primarily concerned with building general character, with liberal education, or with producing the "whole man" but, rather, with scholarship. Depth of knowledge and learning was all im-

---

parative Education," in *Encyclopedia of Educational Research* (1969); Abraham Flexner, *Medical Education: A Comparative Study* (New York: Macmillan, 1925), *Universities: American, English, German* (New York: Oxford, 1930), and *Medical Education in the United States and Canada* (New York: Carnegie Foundation for the Advancement of Teaching, 1910); Nicholas Hans, *Comparative Education: A Study of Educational Factors and Traditions* (London: Routledge and Kegan Paul, 1949); Franz Hilker, *Vergleichende Pädagogik* . . . (Munich: Hueber, 1962); Isaac L. Kandel, *Comparative Education* (Boston: Houghton Mifflin, 1933); Paul Monroe, *Essays in Comparative Education* (New York: Teachers College, Columbia University, 1927 and 1932); Michael Sadler, "How Far Can We Learn Anything of Practical Value from the Study of Foreign Systems of Education?" (Guildford, Eng.: Printed at the Surrey Advertiser Office, 1900); Peter Sandiford, ed., *Comparative Education: Studies of the Educational Systems of Six Modern Nations* (London: Dent, 1918); Friedrich Schneider, *Vergleichende Erziehungswissenschaft* (Heidelberg; Quelle and Meyer, 1961); Charles H. Thurber, *The Principles of School Organization* (Worcester: Oliver B. Wood, 1900).

138

portant, and the professor was supreme, nearly infallible, and well-nigh untouchable.

In the United States, the situation was, of course, in several important respects, very different. Following the American Revolution, the idea of complete equality of all, including equality and democracy in education, became a cornerstone of the new nation. To be sure, there were still those, Jefferson among them, in positions of importance who retained the English elitist notion of education but, by the time of the Jacksonian democracy the ideal of equality in education was almost universally accepted. Equally early was the notion that higher education should serve useful and practical purposes. Though the idea came to full flower only with the creation of the land-grant colleges and universities after mid-century, it was expressed by Franklin and was present even in the stated purposes of the colonial colleges, which trained for the ministry and teaching.

The rapid growth in national wealth and in industrialization, together with the expanding western frontier, combined to accelerate the development of mass education and to increase its practical nature at the college and, later, university level. It was not long after the founding of the first real university in the United States, the Johns Hopkins University in 1876, that universities, led by Cornell, were offering instruction in almost any subject that anyone wanted to learn, including some of exceedingly dubious academic legitimacy.

All of this—grossly oversimplified and omitting far more than it includes—reflects the national character or *Volksgeist* of the peoples and their political, sociological, economic, and cultural history, and has influenced the nature of university libraries of the three countries. The facts that books may not be taken out of the Bodleian Library of Oxford University; that in German universities students have no access to the stacks and they generally pay for their call slips, and that the often large and always numerous, non-circulating, restricted-access institute and seminar libraries frequently have more books and money than

139

the university library; and that, in the United States, large numbers of duplicate copies of books are bought for students' required and collateral reading are reflections of national histories.

In short, one cannot effectively study the university libraries of the three countries without understanding the history which made them what they are.

If comparative librarianship is considered as a *total subject*, as described in chapter 2, its methodology is also determined by the objective which a particular investigation is intended to meet. As noted in other connections in chapters 2 and 4, the purpose of learning something *about* the libraries, or some aspect of librarianship in some country or region, is a wholly legitimate one, and all that is needed here is a description—without explanation, without a search for cause and effect, without any effort to arrive at generalizations—based upon a careful collection of all possible relevant data. As also discussed in chapters 2 and 4, such a collection and description are, indeed, an absolutely essential first step—after establishment of the hypothesis—in any comparative study, whether the step be taken by the one who makes the study, or whether it has already been taken by someone else, but it does not constitute in itself a comparative study. Such a study requires the investigator to search for information not only about but, more important, *into* the phenomena he has studied, that is, to seek to learn what factors determined the nature of the phenomena, and what conditions have accounted for the differences. The point could hardly be better put than Noah and Eckstein have made it for education:

> The scholar who collects data on, say, teacher-training practices for European secondary education, arranges them in convenient categories, discusses the validity of the categories and the reliability of the information, and goes no further, is stopping short just at the point where comparative *investigation* begins. He can, and often does, sug-

gest tentative explanations for some of the phenomena he has uncovered, but it is the precise formulation of hypotheses, discussion of the theoretical justifications for advancing them, and the statement and operationalizing of concepts and indicators that represent the essence of comparative work in education. It goes far beyond the business of assembling data simply for infomational purposes, important and difficult though even that task may be.[22]

Franz Hilker advances the same basic contention:

The careful, grounded presentation of foreign school systems and the juxtaposition of such systems, or of particular problems of a . . . foreign school system in spatial or chronological differentiation is not comparison. Such presentation can be a preliminary step to comparison, but it lacks a determining characteristic which is essential for comparison, namely, explanation. The aim of comparison is not simply the collection of material in clear order, but rather the *winning of new knowledge* which is possible only through this means.[23]

In fact, virtually every comparativist in the social sciences has made the same two points: the absolute essentiality of the accurate collection and careful description and analysis of facts as the first stage of all comparative studies, and the fact that such collection and description do not, in themselves, constitute comparison, even when the phenomena described are cross-societal.[24]

It is important to emphasize here a consideration far too often ignored in area studies in librarianship. This is that even though such studies are neither comparative nor cross-societal, it is still

[22] Noah and Eckstein, *Comparative Education*, pp. 187–88.

[23] Hilker, *Vergleichende Pädagogik*, p. 65 (my translation).

[24] See also, for example, Robert G. Templeton, "Some Reflections on the Theory of Comparative Education," *Comparative Education Review* 2:28 (Oct. 1958).

141

essential that they be inter-disciplinary. The description, or the description and analysis, of an area or a problem, situation, or type of library within it, by means of only the single discipline, librarianship, is not an area study. Clearly, no a priori list can be set down of the other disciplines of which account must be taken; the nature of the particular study is here determinant. But history is indispensable, education and sociology will generally be involved, and economics, geography, and political science are frequently important.[25]

It has already been pointed out that comparative librarianship, or what commonly passes for it, has only very infrequently gone "beyond the business of assembling data simply for informational purposes." Seldom have comparative librarianship studies had as their aim the provision of validated explanation of variations in development, practice, and status of librarianship in different cultures, and even less often have the results of the studies been assessed, or tested for reliability. This means, in effect, that a primary, if not the primary goal of comparative study in any field has, with us, been almost wholly neglected. To quote Noah and Eckstein again:

> Systematic, controlled, empirical, and (wherever possible) quantitative investigation of explicitly stated hypotheses is the hallmark of the contemporary social sciences. . . . To the extent that the investigator in cross-national research is crystal-clear in his own mind and makes quite clear to his readers, precisely which hypothetical proposition he is testing, he furnishes himself with a focus for research and his readers with a clear guide to understanding the implications of the results achieved. However, to the extent that work using cross-national educational data is unsystematic, lacks explicit controls, appeals for proof to authority or

[25] The argument for a general "social science perspective" in comparative education studies is made by W. J. Siffin, "The Social Sciences, Comparative Education, the Future, and All That," *Comparative Education Review* 13:252–59 (Oct. 1969).

intuition rather than to the facts, and ignores possibilities of quantification of variables, it is poor social science and therefore poor comparative education.[26]

Very little that flies under the flag of comparative librarianship meets these essential criteria.

Too frequently, in fact, in librarianship, the collection of data has been confused and identified with research and, when cross-societal, with comparison. The result is that the publication of almost any aggregation of facts has been described with one or both of those words. Data collection, whether done by the investigator himself, or by someone else, is an indispensable step in research and is essential for the testing of any hypothesis. But mere compilation, no matter how accurate and comprehensive, is not research. It is the analysis and treatment of the facts, and the conclusions and explanations that this analysis enables one to draw that, together, justify one in speaking of a piece of research.

The value of explanation probably does not need argument or demonstration, but an illustration may be useful. Beginning with the founding of Johns Hopkins University, the American university and its library adopted, almost lock, stock, and barrel, the concepts and practices of their German counterparts. The seminar (Lehr- und Lernfreiheit), the basic requirements for the doctor's degree, and the departmental library were derived directly from Germany. In one major respect, at least, our library practice differed radically from that of Germany. By the end of the nineteenth century, book selection for the university library in that country was entirely in the hands of library staff; in the United States it was almost entirely in the hands of the faculty, and it remained there, generally speaking, until the 1960s. If we had understood clearly why we departed so radically in this respect from our German model and had carefully tested the results of the two practices, it seems probable that we would have

[26] Noah and Eckstein, Comparative Education, p. 186.

moved much earlier than we did toward adoption of book selection by library staff.

In this general connection, another major observation is necessary. One looks in vain anywhere for criteria upon which to judge the quality of work in comparative librarianship. Such criteria are desperately needed. They are needed by students and others who read the literature and must judge its value. They are in the same way needed by journal editors. They are needed by library school faculty. They are needed by planners faced with studies purporting to offer solutions to problems. And they are needed by those whose own research efforts require them to judge whether the published work of someone else is good or not. It is probably beyond the capacity of anyone today to say specifically what these criteria should be. But if we faithfully follow the routes and accepted methodological techniques and practices of the other social disciplines which have had a long experience in comparative studies, if we rigorously adhere to these techniques, and if we then judge our own work by the standards commonly applied in the evaluation of such studies, we are not likely to go far wrong.

The difficulties in, and the deterrents to, the adoption of the methods and techniques discussed thus far are numerous, and they should not be ignored or lightly passed over. Some of them have been earlier implied.

1. Such data and information about libraries as we now have vary enormously in their comprehensiveness, accuracy, reliability, recency, and nature. We may find, for instance, full and accurate information about annual book purchases or use of one kind of library in this or that country, but not in others, or not for certain years.

2. Speaking multi-nationally, our concepts are often poorly or not at all defined. In the preceding paragraph, for example, how books are counted differs from country to country, and occasionally even between libraries of the same country. Does "purchase" include books for branch, departmen-

tal, and institute libraries, or only the "main" library of a university? What constitutes library "use?"

3. All cross-societal comparisons involving financial data face two difficulties that call for special care and particular knowledge. The first concerns currency differences and their reconciliation to a common base; the second, differences in purchasing power. If we were to determine, for instance, that libraries of a certain kind in an Eastern European and a Western European country had the same amounts of money to spend for the purchase of books, the two groups of libraries would not be able to buy the same number of volumes published in the West. The same budgets for salaries make possible the employment of more librarians in Italy or Spain than in West Germany or Sweden. In like manner, libraries far distant from the principal publication centers of Western Europe, North America, and the USSR, which must add expensive transportation charges to their book costs, will not be able to purchase as many volumes for the same amount of money as libraries located near those centers. To determine how many fewer is difficult and time-consuming. More difficult still is the problem of reducing to a common base the value, say, of the Czech krone, the German mark, and the British pound for 1946. The greater the distance in time from the immediate present of a study, the greater will be the difficulty in reconciling different currencies and determining purchasing power.

4. The avoidance of bias, whether external or built-in, presents a particularly difficult problem in the social sciences and, because of our strong humanistic and non-scientifically oriented tradition, the problem is especially acute in librarianship. The conscientious and "objective" investigator can presumably avoid the error of attempting to prove a case for the superiority or the inferiority of some practice or procedure, either in his own country or another. But it is less easy to rid oneself of an unconscious conviction that this way or that way is the only satisfactory one. The unconsciously held a priori judgment is likely to impose techniques of inquiry and data selection, and conclusions,

145

influenced by professional, national, or even personal values assumed to be the "right" ones.

5. Bias is inherent in and, to some extent, ineradicable from the data selection process in most social studies. Every investigator comes to such a study with his own particular background, which results in certain predilections, interests, points of view, beliefs, and the like. Unless he uses extraordinary care and objectivity, his selection of certain facts and rejection of others is likely to be adversely influenced.

6. An equally serious and difficult problem arises from the subconscious or even willful misrepresentation of data published by individuals, private agencies, and governments. Consider, for example, the matter of library reports of whatever kind. For some kinds of data and some kinds of investigation, these are frequently the most nearly "primary" source available to an investigator, for he cannot reconstruct the past history which produced them, and should he turn to the reporting individual or agency, he is likely to find that the actual primary data, from which the report was created, were discarded when the report appeared, and are no longer available. Reports, however, have the wholly legitimate purpose, in part, of demonstrating the need for additional financial or other kinds of support, and they may be expected not to place the library's accomplishments and operations in the worst possible light. Accordingly, even though the data reported may be arithmetically and factually accurate, the slant and emphasis given to them, the selection-inclusion of some and the rejection-omission of other data may produce a result or impression quite different from reality. The reports of school library systems, which depend on state aid for support; of university libraries, the amount of use of which may be a factor in determining the level of support; and of governments, where considerations of national prestige play a role, may all be colored, and such coloration is extraordinarily difficult to ascertain.

7. A further difficulty, faced by comparative investigators in the social sciences generally, is the too easy assumption

that what appears to be the same condition or situation in two societies really is so. This goes far beyond such a relatively simple matter as the incorrect translation of the German word *Hochschule*, or the French *école secondaire*, by the (American) English "high school," or even the assumption that *öffentliche Bibliothek* (public library) carries the same conditions and meaning as the "free public library" in the understanding of the Anglo-American and Scandinavian worlds. Almost every concept must be vigorously dissected and tested for its real meaning against the history, tradition, and social milieu of the society in which it is found.

8. We need to remember that, however rigorously and "scientifically" we collect and treat library data, the comparative method with us, as in most social disciplines, is at present, and is likely to remain for a long time, an imperfect substitute for the kind of experimentation available to the physical scientist.

9. Comparative librarianship is gravely handicapped, as other disciplines first entering upon real comparative study have been, by an almost total lack of information about results, effects, and products. We can find, for example, for some kinds of libraries in some societies that they lent so many volumes a year, but we have an almost total absence of data on the reasons for their being borrowed, on the extent to which these volumes were actually read or used, the results of their use, the kinds of people who borrowed them—to say nothing of why other or different sorts of people did not borrow books. To say that every British citizen has easy access to wholly free public library service, however admirable the fact is, tells us a great deal more about British society than it does about how the British public library works, or the effects of its efforts. One may ask—but one asks in vain—whether an often avowed aim of the American public library, namely to aid in the creation and maintenance of an enlightened citizenry has, in fact, had any effect whatever on, for example, the voting record of Americans.

147

10. Finally, in a somewhat different vein, mention should be made, and stress laid upon, the less tangible problems created by radically differing cultural viewpoints and attitudes in individual countries. The point here is that major difficulties in comparative study are frequently related to religious belief, traditional class structure, or deeply rooted systems of values. When one or more of these differs materially from traditional Western ones, the effect often is that many of the basic ideas underlying modern concepts of library support, administration, and service produce serious cultural shock in the people concerned. Although this is particularly the case in many developing countries, it is also not infrequently apparent in some countries generally considered developed. The comparativist must be alert to recognize profound cultural differences and the *Weltanschauung* of a country; if he does not, he cannot successfully study it.

In this century, especially after World War I and most particularly since World War II, the explanatory powers of the social sciences have been markedly strengthened. This has resulted in part from the development of vastly improved statistical techniques, in part from improvement in the quantity and quality of data collected and made available by governmental and nongovernmental agencies. Simply as instances here, for the field of education, one may cite the United States Office of Education which, in fact, itself began research in comparative education as early as 1878 and issues, among other publications, a bulletin and a series, Studies in Comparative Education; the *Educational Yearbook* (1924–44) of Teachers College, Columbia University; the Institute of Education of the University of London and its *Yearbook of Education;* the Comparative Education Center in the Department of Education of the University of Chicago; the University of Munich and the *International Education Review* founded in 1930 by Friedrich Schneider; the UNESCO Institute for Education founded in 1951 at the University of

Hamburg; the *Hochschule für Internationale Pädagogische Forschung* established in 1949 at Frankfurt; the Institute of Educational Sciences at the University of Geneva; the Max Planck Institute for Educational Research in West Berlin; the *Institut für Vergleichende Erziehungswissenschaft* in Salzburg; the *Dokumentations- und Informationszentrum* in Bonn, an establishment of the Permanent Conference of the Ministers of Education of the Federal Republic of Germany; the *Institut Pédagogique National* and its *Musée Pédagogique*, in Paris; the (UNESCO) International Bureau of Education established in 1925 in Geneva, which maintains a large documentation center in comparative and international education and publishes a quarterly bulletin and *The International Yearbook of Education*; and, of course, UNESCO itself. Reference to comparable data-gathering, research, and publication centers in Belgium, Brazil, Colombia, India, Italy, Japan, the Netherlands, Sweden, the USSR, and elsewhere could easily increase this listing several times. Similar citations could be made for other social sciences.

It has been possible, accordingly, to ground contemporary cross-national and cross-societal study in education upon two bases: improved and sophisticated statistical and other techniques in social science research on the one hand, and enormously increased bodies of available data on the other. The development of work in comparative librarianship will have to be founded on the same two bases. This will require, first, the use or adaptation of the methods and techniques of the social sciences; and, second, a great increase in all kinds of library data, including solid, carefully gathered and analyzed information about aspects of librarianship in many countries—in other words, area studies.

With very few, relatively small-scale, exceptions—such as the library activities of the United States Office of Education, and the International Library Information Center, Graduate School of Library and Information Sciences, University of Pittsburgh—

comparative librarianship lacks sources and centers such as education has.[27] Some of what is available in education and the other social sciences is of utility to the student of comparative librarianship, and the bibliography compiled by Simsova and MacKee includes most of the major present sources of library data of relevance to it.[28]

[27] The Center at the University of Pittsburgh is possibly the most comprehensive anywhere. It contains (1972) about 11,000 items in 33 languages from 142 countries, and includes library annual reports; material on standards, statistics, and legislation; newspaper and journal articles; conference proceedings; dissertations; studies; and surveys.

[28] S. Simsova and M. MacKee, *A Handbook of Comparative Librarianship* (London: Bingley, c1970), pp. 57–370.

6

Envoi

To one who is concerned about comparative librarianship, who —if only on the basis of the tremendous contributions which have been made by comparative studies in other disciplines— firmly believes that the progress of librarianship as a whole would be substantially furthered by more and more serious attention to it, and who dispassionately views the present state of the art, the situation today is discouraging. It is not, however, by any means hopeless.

We have, in several countries in the world, major universities which have strong programs in both library education and comparative studies in the social sciences. In a number of countries, as briefly noted in chapters 1 and 5, we have significant institutional, governmental, and international agencies specifically concerned with librarianship or comparative education, or both. And there is around the world an increasing corps of librarians with international interests and educational background, language facility, and experience. Finally, the still relatively few and

still largely elementary-level programs in comparative librarianship at some library schools and similar agencies have nevertheless begun, during the past decade or so, to produce librarians
with at least some indoctrination in the area. It seems not too
much to hope that from all of this we might, with cautious
optimism, look forward to a serious, productive development of
the field. Among the measures likely to aid in bringing this development to reality—the first is believed to be a *sine qua non*—
are:

1. The establishment at a few major, research-oriented library schools and comparable agencies, in or associated with
strong universities, of high-level, adequately staffed and
supported teaching and research programs. Inasmuch as
some countries even in Europe—for instance Austria, Belgium, Italy, Yugoslavia, and Sweden—have no real library
education programs, and many others around the world
maintain them only at an elementary and practitioner level
(with student admission at about the level of completion
of the American junior college, or the European *gymna-
sium/lycée*), the most likely countries at present for the
viable creation of such programs would seem to be Czechoslovakia, Germany, Great Britain, the Soviet Union, and
the United States. But library education in a few other
countries, such as Argentina, Brazil, Canada, Denmark,
India, Israel, Japan, and Poland (with doctoral programs
in librarianship at Wrocław and Warsaw, and work in comparative education at the latter university) have sufficient
potential, both in librarianship and in comparative studies,
to make the development possible in the not too distant
future.

2. Such centers as those just described would, by definition, require first-class library resources, that is, major collections of monographs, journals, reports, surveys, studies, and
so on, not only in international and comparative librarianship, but also in related fields. There are today in a few places
in the world, chiefly in Great Britain and the United States,

very good collections of this sort, but probably not a single one that could be rated as outstanding, and even of the good to very good collections, there are far too few. Some institutions offering graduate work in comparative and international librarianship (and in librarianship generally) have pitifully weak collections of "foreign" library monographs, reports, surveys, and journals.

3. The establishment at all possible library schools and other library education agencies everywhere of at least a minimal program of instruction in international and, particularly, comparative librarianship. This would not necessarily need to be accomplished solely through separate, new courses. The comparative and international approach and content could well be incorporated into many, and probably most, existing courses, as such content is by necessity present in courses like "Foreign National and Trade Bibliography," or "Foreign Government Publications." The purpose of this suggestion is two-fold: first, to make possible the exposure of many more students than at present to library situations in parts of the world other than their own, and thus to make the future librarian less parochial than he now generally is; and, second, as a hoped-for result of this, to interest a larger number of students in further, specialized pursuit of comparative librarianship.

4. Acceptance by some governments of specific responsibility for support and furtherance of the area, through either existing comparative education or library agencies. In the United States, this could be done either though the International Educational Relations Branch of the Division of International Education of the United States Office of Education, or the Office's Bureau of Libraries and Learning Resources or, conceivably, through a joint activity.

The same desideratum could be achieved in Great Britain, Germany, the USSR, and possibly in other countries. Unfortunately, at present, a number of countries with some international commitments at the national level, and with strong centers, particularly in comparative education, have weak research activity, potential, and interest in librarian-

153

ship, or none at all. It is unlikely that government alone in such countries would develop a strong concern for comparative librarianship.

5. The establishment of a journal, more or less comparable to *The International Review of Education*, or the *Comparative Education Review*, the official organ of the Comparative and International Education Society, specifically devoted to comparative librarianship. (It may be observed that not everything published in these two reviews is, strictly speaking, comparative.) Like *The International Review of Education*, it should have an international editorial board and should publish articles in at least three languages, each article with summaries in the other two.

6. The establishment of a yearbook, more or less similar to *The Educational Yearbook*, published between 1924 and 1944 by the International Institute of Teachers College, Columbia University, or *The International Yearbook of Education*, published by the International Bureau of Education in Geneva. The yearbook, too, should have an international editorial board.

7. The establishment in a few countries, preferably as a section or branch of an existing library association, of a Comparative Librarianship Society somewhat similar to the Comparative and International Education Society. Probably very few countries are ready for such a group at present, or could make one viable and productive, but the great contributions and success of the Comparative and International Education Society lead to the belief that a similar group for comparative librarians would be an effective instrument in those countries that are ready for such development. The founding of the International and Comparative Librarianship Group of the (British) Library Association in 1968 was a move in the right direction, but this group, thus far, has shown no interest in serious comparative work. The same can be said of the International Relations Round Table and the International Relations Committee and Office of the American Library Association.

None of this will be achieved overnight and probably little of it can be achieved soon. Substantial obstacles lie in the path, just as serious problems face efforts to study the library and society comparatively—or, indeed, to adopt and adapt the techniques of social science inquiry to comparative librarianship. But as discussed in the latter half of chapter 3, the promise and potential are great. In view of this potential, in view of the increasing need of all those engaged in intellectual activity to know more about what goes on beyond their national boundaries, and in view, especially, of librarianship's need for the principles, understandings, and broad, new knowledge which can be expected to result from comparative studies, it seems fair to conclude that those in a position to work actively toward the achievement of these goals, or some of them, should make serious efforts in that direction.

APPENDIX

Outline for a Course or Seminar in Comparative Librarianship

The outline is intended to be comprehensive in the sense of including all principal topics properly encompassed in the subject. This means that the material would have to be adapted according to the level of instruction (e.g., introductory course, doctoral level seminar) for which it is used; the amount of instructional time available; the needs of students; and, especially in section IV, the particular country or countries covered. With respect to this last, it will be immediately apparent, for example, that some developing countries have no industry (IV.A.4.c), agencies and programs of adult and fundamental education (IV.A.7.e), or film production (IV.A.8.c). The topics of special libraries (IV.B.4.e), professional training programs (IV.B.6.b), and national library plans (IV.B.9.a) are also not relevant for some countries.

For different reasons, the problems presented by multiple races (IV.A.3.b, IV.A.5.d), languages (IV.A.5.a), and religions (IV.A.5.b) are non-existent, or virtually so, in many countries.

157

Unfortunately, it is also all too true that accurate, comprehensive, up-to-date information on many of the topics noted in section IV is often simply not available, either on general national matters or libraries and librarianship. Although this is especially the case with respect to developing countries, the lack is by no means limited to them. Even for some developed countries, hard data regarding the number and qualifications of library personnel in different kinds of libraries, or the number and qualifications of teachers in library education agencies, for instance, are not available. Though these and other kinds of information might be compiled by an experienced investigator with sufficient time and means at his disposal, it is not to be expected that inexperienced students, with very limited time, can do so. Considerations such as these should influence the choice of countries and the kinds of topics to be studied.

Section IV closely parallels at some points an outline for a graduate seminar in comparative librarianship developed by Dorothy Collings, which she began to give at the School of Library Service, Columbia University, 1956. This outline is reproduced in Simsova and McKee, *A Handbook of Comparative Librarianship* (pp. 400–3). The outline given below is more comprehensive and detailed than that developed by Mrs. Collings and includes, as well, in sections I, II, III, V, and VI material not contained in her outline.

Ideally, the course should be spread over a full academic year, the first half of which would be devoted to sections I, II, III, IV, and VI; section IV would be *considered in general, methodological terms only*. The second half of the year would then be devoted to (1) intensive and extensive consideration of librarianship in at least two different countries, preferably in substantially different parts of the world, with such consideration based upon the factors noted in section IV; and (2) the students' selection and prosecution of a topic of quite limited scope for comparative study in two different countries or societies.

It will be at once apparent that no topic of limited scope that

158

a student could satisfactorily prosecute during the course of a semester—or even a year—would require consideration of more than a small fraction of all of the factors outlined in section IV; the totality of what is included there would apply only to an investigation of the entire library scene of a country, a task which would tax the time, resources, and ability of the ablest scholar. The student should be led to determine which of the factors in section IV are of importance to his topic, and why. A course conducted along these lines should give the student a good introduction to the basics of comparative librarianship and of those aspects of international librarianship related to it. This is about all that we can expect most library education agencies to give to most students and it is, in fact, considerably more than is now available in all but a very few library education programs in the world.

It cannot be too strongly emphasized, however, that such a course, no matter how well conducted, is hardly more than a good beginning in the preparation of future scholars and investigators, in the preparation, that is, of those who expect to be real comparativists. What is additionally required for this small but important group is briefly outlined on page 100.

OUTLINE

I. Introduction
   A. Definitions: comparative librarianship; international librarianship; "foreign" librarianship; area studies; the cross-societal, cross-national element
   B. Scope and limitations
      1. Description and analysis of library "systems," or parts of systems, their development, status, and problems in selected countries or societies
         a. Area studies of librarianship in particular countries or societies
         b. Comparative study of selected topics

2. Analysis of potentialities of library development
3. Aspects of international library co-operation (developed in section VI)
   a. Agencies
   b. Activities and accomplishments; publications
   c. Problems and deterrents
4. Limitations of comparative studies

C. Aims, purposes, and values
   1. To discover and explain the differences in analogous library situations in two or more societies (C*)
   2. To study available data concerning the development and status of the library "systems" of selected countries, and their library problems (S**)
   3. To relate such development and status to historical, social, economic, political, geographic, and other pertinent factors (S)
   4. To contribute to the analysis and solution of library problems (C)
   5. To assist in library planning (C)
   6. To stimulate the adoption or adaptation of "better" practices and techniques (C)
   7. To provide information useful in "foreign" work and study assignments (S)
   8. To strengthen the content of library education programs (C)
   9. To gain perspective on, and better understanding of, one's own national library "system" and problems (S)
   10. To assist in the development of data and techniques for the comparative study of library "systems" and problems (C)
   11. To assist in the advancement of better international understanding and co-operation in library development (C)
   12. To indicate needed areas for further development and research at home and abroad (C)

* C = primarily an aim, purpose, or value of comparative studies.
** S = primarily an aim, purpose, or value of the seminar.

13. To provide basic information on "foreign" librarianship and comparative methodology and technique (S)
II. Research, bibliography, and publication
III. Methodology and techniques: scientific method; the nature of comparison; the cross-disciplinary requirement
IV. Outline for the study of a library "system"
   A. General background information
      1. Principal historical determinants
      2. Geography and climate
      3. Sociological factors
         a. Total number of inhabitants
         b. Racial and national composition
         c. Sex and age groups (adults; children of school age; children under 6; population over 65)
         d. Urban-rural distribution; density
         e. Traditional class structure
      4. Economic factors
         a. Sources and amounts of tax and other revenues
         b. National and per capita income; gross national product
         c. Main occupations, industries, and services; percent of population in each; productivity
         d. Cost of living
      5. Cultural factors (see also 7 below)
         a. Languages
         b. Main religions, their status and influence; religious belief; population percentages
         c. Systems of values
         d. Other (e.g., segregation by race or sex)
      6. Political factors
         a. Governmental structure (national, state, local)
         b. Form
         c. Extent of centralization
         d. Political parties
      7. Educational factors
         a. The educational system; number of schools and institutions of higher education per 100,000 population; control; financial support, by level

161

   b. Educational levels—years of schooling completed;
      extent of illiteracy; compulsory education
   c. Percent and number of school-age children in school
   d. Students in higher education—number and percent
   e. Agencies and programs of adult and fundamental
      education (e.g., agricultural extension services; liter-
      acy programs)
   f. Structure of and education for the professions
8. Media of communication
   a. Number and circulation of newspapers
   b. Production and distribution of books and magazines;
      book stores
   c. Film production and attendance
   d. Radio and television
B. The library "system"
   1. Historical review
      a. Library tradition and historic beginnings
      b. Landmarks in library development
      c. Numbers and types of libraries (See also B.4)
   2. Current statements of library objectives and standards
   3. Library government
      a. National responsibilities for library service
         i. Laws and legislation
         ii. Financial support or assistance
         iii. Control and supervision
         iv. Centralized services to libraries
         v. Other direct or special services
      b. The role of state, province, and municipality in li-
         brary development
      c. Local responsibilities for library services
   4. Library resources: number, income, staff, holdings,
      buildings, services, and use
      a. National and state libraries
      b. Public libraries
      c. School libraries
      d. Academic libraries
      e. Special libraries

      f. "Foreign" libraries (e.g., British Council, United States Information Service)

5. Library materials (extent and characteristics)
    a. Books and pamphlets
    b. Periodicals and newspapers
    c. Government publications
    d. Films and other audio-visual materials
    e. Materials for children and young people
    f. Special problems
       i. Language problems
      ii. Materials for illiterate and newly literate adults
     iii. Other (e.g., books for the blind)

6. Library personnel and training
    a. Existing library personnel
       i. Number and qualifications; number per capita
      ii. Salaries and status *vis à vis* other professions
     iii. Associations
    b. Professional training programs
       i. Origin and number
      ii. Academic level(s)
     iii. Curricula
     iv. Certification and degrees
      v. Materials and methods of instruction
     vi. Teaching staff—number and qualifications
    vii. Library resources
   viii. Research and publications
    c. Apprenticeship and other in-service training programs
    d. "Foreign" study and visitation
       i. Opportunities for, and extent of, "foreign" study
      ii. Equivalences of "foreign" study programs
     iii. Advantages and limitations of study abroad

7. Library service
    a. By type of library
    b. By type of user
       i. Children
      ii. Students

iii. General adult population

iv. Special groups (e.g., minorities, prisoners, physically handicapped, hospital patients, business and professional people)

   c. Reference and information service

8. Means, tools, techniques

   a. Acquisitions—centralized, specialized, cooperative (e.g., the acquisition and processing centers of the Scandinavian countries; the Scandia, Farmington, and West German *Sondersammelgebiete* Plans; National Program for Acquisitions and Cataloging; copyright deposit)

   b. National and trade bibliography; bibliographical control

   c. Cataloging and cooperative cataloging

   d. Classification schemes

   e. Loan, especially interlibrary

9. Aspects of library development

   a. Analysis of existing national or other library plans and studies

   b. Library coverage: quantitative; qualitative

     i. Size, types, and dissemination of library units

     ii. Library co-ordination and co-operation

   c. Library finances

     i. National, state, and local

     ii. Other (e.g., philanthropic foundations)

   d. Library buildings and equipment

   e. Library personnel and training

     i. Professional

     ii. Other

   f. International relations and opportunities for international assistance and co-operation

     i. Exchange or training of library personnel

     ii. Operation of demonstration or other field programs

     iii. Supply (including translations or adaptations) of publications, films, or other materials

     iv. Grants-in-aid or other financial assistance

  10. Summary and recommendations
    a. Main characteristics and achievements of the library system
    b. Outstanding problems and needs
    c. Suggested topics for research and investigation
  11. Selected bibliography (systematic listing of main sources of information, including statistical data)
V. Comparative study of selected topics in the fields of
  A. Education of librarians
  B. Academic librarianship
  C. School and children's library service
  D. Public librarianship
  E. National and state libraries
  F. Special libraries
VI. International library co-operation and support
  A. Agencies
    1. UNESCO and other international bodies
    2. IFLA, FID, INTAMEL and other library associations
    3. National government agencies (e.g., national libraries; British Council; USIS; AID)
    4. Philanthropic foundations (e.g., Carnegie, Ford, Gulbenkian, Rockefeller)
    5. Library schools
    6. Other (e.g., university and other libraries)
  B. Activities
    1. Education and training of library personnel
    2. Demonstration projects (e.g., New Delhi Public Library)
    3. "Foreign" field programs
    4. Conferences and other meetings
    5. Publications
    6. International exchanges
    7. Other
  C. Problems and deterrents
    1. Program planning
    2. Finance
    3. Personnel
    4. Fact-finding and research

165

5. Translation and adaptation of materials
6. Co-ordination of resources and services
7. Geographical distance
8. Language
9. Differences in current practices—vested interests
10. Differences in class structures, religious beliefs, and value systems.
11. Inertia

Bibliography

Included here are all of the writings about comparative/international librarianship referred to in chapters 2 and 3, as well as other publications on the subject not pertinent to the purposes of those two chapters.

Comparative and international studies themselves, area studies, surveys, reports, and other writing about librarianship in different countries are not included. Most such writing, until about 1970, is noted in the extensive "Guide to Sources," in Simsova and MacKee's *A Handbook of Comparative Librarianship* (pp. 57–370).

Asheim, Lester. *Librarianship in the Developing Countries.* Urbana: Univ. of Illinois Pr., 1966.

Bevis, Dorothy. "Libraries and People—Worldwide." *Journal of Education for Librarianship* 10:159–65 (Winter 1970).

Brewster, Beverly J. "International Library School Programs." *Journal of Education for Librarianship* 9:138–43 (Fall 1968).

Burnett, A. David. "The Problems of Comparing the Library Service of Different Countries." Sevensma prize paper of the International Federation of Library Associations, 1971.

Campbell, H. C. "Internationalism in U.S. Library School Curricula." *International Library Review* 2:183–86 (Apr. 1970).

Carroll, Frances Laverne. "International Education for Librarianship." *International Library Review* 2:19–39 (Jan. 1970).

Chandler, George. "International and Comparative Librarianship." In his *Libraries in the East: An International and Comparative Study*, pp. 1–17. London: Seminar Pr., 1971.

Despite its title, the first chapter of Chandler's book is not about either international or comparative librarianship; instead, it is a partial summary of certain aspects of librarianship in the eight Near Eastern and Asian countries that the author visited in 1970. The work as a whole is not at all comparative, but simply a narrative account, country by country, of various kinds of libraries and of aspects of librarianship.

Cleeve, Marigold. "International and Comparative Librarianship Group 1967–1968." *International Library Review* 1:93–96 (Jan. 1969).

Collings, Dorothy G. "Comparative Librarianship." *Encyclopedia of Library and Information Science* 5:492–502.

———. "Meeting the Needs of Foreign Students." *Library Journal* 83:3064–66 (Nov. 1 1958).

———. "Training Overseas Students in American Library Schools." *UNESCO Bulletin for Libraries* 13:180–83 (Aug.-Sept. 1959).

Dane, Chase. "The Benefits of Comparative Librarianship." *The Australian Library Journal* 3:89–91 (July 1954).

———. "Comparative Librarianship." *The Librarian and Book World* 43:141–44 (Aug. 1954).

Foskett, D. J. "Comparative Librarianship." *The Library World* 66:295–98 (June 1965).

———. "Comparative Librarianship." In *Progress in Library Science, 1965*, edited by Robert L. Collison, pp. 125–46. London: Butterworths, 1965.

———. "Comparative Classification." In his *Science, Humanism, and Libraries*, pp. 179–90. London: Lockwood, c. 1964.

Harrison, K. C. Quoted by Marigold Cleeve, "International and

Comparative Librarianship 1967–1968." *International Library Review* 1:95 (Jan. 1969).

Hassenforder, Jean. "Comparative Studies and the Development of Public Libraries." *UNESCO Bulletin for Libraries* 22:13–19 (Jan.-Feb. 1968).

Jackson, Miles M., Jr. "Libraries Abroad." *The Journal of Library History* 1:133–34 (Apr. 1966).

"The Research Rationale for International Comparative Librarianship." Discussion paper presented at a faculty conference of the New York State University, held at Oyster Bay, N.Y., 1966. Processed.

Roe, John. "International and Comparative Librarianship Activities." *Library Association Record* 72:266–67 (July 1970).

Sable, Martin H. and Lourdes Deya. "Outline of an Introductory Course in International and Comparative Librarianship." *International Library Review* 2:187–92 (Apr. 1970).

Sharify, Nasser. "Beyond the National Frontiers: The International Dimension of Changing Library Education for a Changing World." Paper presented to the Committee on Library Education at the General Council Meeting of the International Federation of Library Associations, 30 August 1972, at Budapest. Mimeographed.

———. "The Need for Change in Present Library Science Curricula." In *Library Education: An International Survey*, edited by Larry E. Bone, pp. 171–96. Champaign: Univ. of Illinois Graduate School of Library Science, 1968.

——— and Roland R. Piggford, "First Institute on International Comparative Librarianship. . . ." *Pennsylvania Library Association Bulletin* 21:73–80 (Nov. 1965).

Shores, Louis. *Around the Library World in 76 Days.* Berkeley, Calif.: Peacock Pr., 1967.

———. "Comparative Librarianship: A Theoretical Approach." In *Comparative and International Librarianship*, edited by Miles M. Jackson, Jr., pp. 3–24. Westport, Conn.: Greenwood, 1970.

———. "Librarian, Know Yourself." *Canadian Library Journal* 27:450–54 (Nov.-Dec. 1970).

———. "Public Library U.S.A.: An Essay in Comparative Librarianship." In *Libraries for the People: International Studies in Librarianship in Honour of Lionel R. McColvin, C.B.E., F.L.A.,* edited by Robert F. Vollans, pp. 239–56. London: Library Assn., 1968.

————. "Why Comparative Librarianship?" *Wilson Library Bulletin* 41:200–06 (Oct. 1966).

Simsova, Sylvia. "The Problems of Comparing the Library Service of Different Countries." Sevensma prize paper, second-place, of the International Federation of Library Associations, 1971.

———— and M. C. MacKee, *A Handbook of Comparative Librarianship.* London: Bingley, c. 1970.

Thompson, Anthony. "Towards International Comparative Librarianship." *Journal of Librarianship* 4:57–69 (Jan. 1972).

White, Carl M. "Comparative Study of Library Systems." In *Bases of Modern Librarianship . . . ,* edited by Carl M. White, pp. 13–26. Oxford: Pergamon Pr., 1964.

170

Index

171

International and Comparative Librarianship Group. See Library Association (Gt. Brit.), International and Comparative Librarianship Group

International Association of Universities Bulletin, m24

International Bureau of Education, m24, 149, 154

International Conference on Cataloguing Principles (1961), m3, 77

International Congress of Comparative Law (1924), m13

International education. See Education, international

International Education Review, m148

International Federation of Library Associations (IFLA), m2

IFLA Annual . . . , m2

Proceedings, m2

International Institute of Statistics (Vienna), m19

International Journal of Adult and Youth Education, m24

International law, use of term, m53

International librarianship, 44–45

defined, 53, 54

definitions of, quoted, 37–39

history of, 1–3

literature of, 85–94

usefulness of, 93–94

International Library Review, 42; q105

International Relations Board (of ALA). See American

Library Association, International Relations Committee

International Relations Committee (of ALA). See American Library Association, International Relations Committee

International Relations Office (of ALA). See American Library Association, International Relations Office

International Relations Round Table (of ALA). See American Library Association, International Relations Round Table

International Review of Education, m22, 24, 154

International Standard Bibliographic Description, m77

International studies and American universities, 98–99

International studies and comparative studies compared, 38–39, 41–42

International understanding and comparative studies, 77

International Yearbook of Education, m149, 154

Intuition, 112

Italy, m24, 149, 152

Jackson, Miles M., Jr., 32; q32, 67–68

Jackson, William Vernon. *Aspects of Librarianship in Latin America,* 92

Jakobson, Roman. *Fundamentals of Language,* m10

Japan, m24, 149, 152

Jefferson, Thomas, m139